Repurpose Your Career:

A Practical Guide

For the Second Half of Life

Marc Miller

With Susan Lahey

Repurpose Your Career
A Practical Guide for the Second Half of Life

ISBN 978-0-9887005-2-9

PRAISE FOR REPURPOSE YOUR CAREER: A PRACTICAL GUIDE FOR THE SECOND HALF OF LIFE

Repurpose Your Career *provides jobseekers of all ages with essential information and action steps that can transform their lives. The book should be seen as survival gear. It will help you navigate the deep questions such as: Do you even know what your talents are? What makes you love one job and not another? Do you know how to describe the kinds of environments that put you "in the zone" from a work perspective? As Miller writes: "People tend to look at jobs from the perspective of salary and benefits but there are so many other things that matter."*

Kerry Hannon, Work and Jobs Expert, author of *Love Your Job: The New Rules of Career Happiness and Getting The Job You Want After 50*

How can I find purpose and a paycheck in my next act? Figuring out what comes next is a journey. Marc Miller offers practical guidance and informed advice for anyone looking for both meaning and money in the second half of life.

Chris Farrell, author of *Unretirement*

If you're ready to pivot to a better career, don't miss the revised edition of Repurpose Your Career. *It's an up-to-date guide that is filled with captivating stories and step-by-step strategies for taking control of your career - and your life. Smart, sensible and action-oriented, this is an important read.*

Nancy Collamer, Semi-Retirement Expert and Founder of MyLifestyleCareer.com

Marc Miller's guide is a highly useful roadmap for anyone who'd like to make a career pivot. Its timely, practical tips on strategic networking, job hunting and building a personal brand are first-rate for the second half of life.

Richard Eisenberg, Work & Purpose Editor, *PBS Nextavenue.org*

Career transitions are challenging, particularly in today's increasingly complex work environment. In Repurpose Your Career, *Marc Miller proposes a compelling and insightful set of practices that anyone can use to pivot from a long-held career to new opportunities and a sustainable second-act.*

John Tarnoff, Reinvention Career Coach, author of *Boomer Reinvention: How to Create Your Dream Career Over 50*

The disruption we're experiencing in when, where, how, and even why we work means many of us are reevaluating our goals, choices, and futures. And that disruption affects us all in different ways, forcing many to ask what's next? Is this it? or How did I wind up here? Everyone from baby boomers to gen X, to even millennials, will find inspiration from the advice and actionable tips Marc offers in the second edition of Repurpose Your Career. *Read this book to find your own answer to the question, what's next?*

Brie Weiler Reynolds, Senior Career Specialist at FlexJobs

Most people know how jobs are filled. Few know how to execute a career pivot. To change direction and earn our living doing the things we really enjoy and are good at. To do this, we must know ourselves better. What we have, what we seek and what we need. Marc is my favorite expert on this vital life skill. And it requires a scientific approach to execute successfully. Marc's own life and experiences have given him all the qualifications needed to understand and explain how we can all find meaningful and rewarding work in the 21st century. Better still, if you follow the advice he presents so clearly here, you'll never hate your work again.

Neil Patrick, Editor: 40pluscareerguru.blogspot.co.uk

Marc dismantles any notion of the hands-off approach to your career. It is contrary to much of the traditional job search advice. You're the advocate and catalyst of your career. If you rather take part in a passive approach to your career, then skip this book. The most relevant career advice in 2017 is you driving engagement with people online and off, keeping the relationship fires stoked — employed or not —, and being empowered pilot opportunities before investing the best of your ideas into a career. A job search in 2017 without networking is like cereal without milk.

Mark Anthony Dyson, founder of "The Voice of Job Seekers" blog and podcast

As we all progress through our life journey, there may be times where we find ourselves stuck in situations that are suboptimal to fulfilling our life purpose. In this book, Marc Miller provides valuable insight on how to recognize the need for change and how to quickly leap back on to the road of success.

L. Xavier Cano, aka The Resume Whiz®

FOREWORD
BY KATHY LANSFORD-POWELL

Do you know this person? Are you this person?

With great anticipation, he/she accepted a job right out of school, vigorously worked to exceed expectations, impress boss and coworkers, and move up in the organization only to discover years later that the job seemed pointless, the politics stifling, and that profits counted more than service. To make matters worse, family responsibilities, financial obligations, need for benefits, lack of marketable skills, or even aversion to change meant that this unfulfilling, soulless employment could conceivably last another twenty or even thirty years.

Sometimes layoff or termination brings an abrupt and unexpected end to the misery, but job loss is usually accompanied by a rash of new problems: financial constraints, family pressure, a flood of debilitating emotions, the urgent need to acquire job search skills, and the overarching imperative—figuring out what to be next.

Marc Miller is a Subject Matter Expert on figuring out what to be next. By choice or circumstance, he has reinvented himself and repurposed his career multiple times, each time learning valuable lessons about himself, his talents, and what he needs in a job to be optimally happy, healthy, and productive. In this easy-to-read book, Marc has demonstrated one of his most significant revelations: the importance of helping others. The career journey isn't one we take alone. The more people we can help along the way, the easier it will be for us to make changes with the support of others. Miller takes the reader by the hand, acknowledging his apprehension and bewilderment, and guides him step-by-step through a multi-faceted process of self-analysis, searching for the moments of clarity, the trail markers, that will show the way to a purposeful career. As expressed in the book, it is a "crazy journey from where we are through ourselves and out the other side to a new beginning," yet one does not have to be a contortionist to reach the goal.

An important element of the career pivot is changing one's mindset. Once mastered, this ability to reframe a situation can be applied not only to the job search but to life in general. Don't look for a job out of desperation; instead, take the time to explore opportunities that will utilize your talents and what you love, or choose to join a company whose mission you wholeheartedly support. In either case, you plot the course. Another dictum from the book, "Don't run away from something—run to something." The book empowers the reader not to feel like a victim, but to be totally in control of the process of reinvention.

the consistent thread running throughout the book is the admonition to ask for help and then help others. "Stop being the expert with twenty years' experience and become the novice asking for help," another piece of job search advice that should be projected onto the big screen of life itself. Expand your network and heed their advice; assemble your tribe of people you can count on; and be alert to opportunities to help others with no thought of personal gain.

A unique aspect of this job search book is the actions listed at the end of each chapter. Repurposing one's career is not a spectator event. It requires thought and homework and action and a sense of urgency. You want to do something you love? Something that has meaning? Time's a-wasting. Get busy.

The collaboration of Marc Miller and Susan Lahey continues to delight. The book instructs us to always show gratitude. Thanks to you both for an excellent roadmap.

Kathy Lansford-Powell
Founder and President of Launch Pad Job Club

HOW TO USE THIS BOOK

This is not the type of book that should be read, cover-to-cover, in a sitting. You probably could read the whole thing in a few hours, but then you wouldn't get the most out of it.

Every chapter has specific insights that I hope will spur specific reflections and actions. I hope you read a chapter at a time, put the book down, reflect back on your career, execute on the action steps and then move on to the next chapter. I encourage you to take notes, highlight sections and move through the book thoughtfully. Those of us in the 2nd half of life have volumes of experience to draw upon, ponder and learn from. Take the time to reflect back upon those experiences.

To really get the most out of this book could take weeks or months. You might even want to read it several times.

At the end of each chapter is a set of action steps. There will be a link to the Repurpose Your Career Resource Center, where you will find copies of the action steps in Microsoft Word format along with a variety of worksheets and other resources to assist you in your journey. To gain access to the Resource Center I ask for your email. This is just so that, as I update information monthly or quarterly, I can keep you informed.

In other words, it's great if you get insights from reading this book, but you'll get so much more if you use it as a tool to inspire reflection, action and growth.

REPURPOSE YOUR CAREER: A PRACTICAL GUIDE FOR THE SECOND HALF OF LIFE

Table of Contents

NEXT UP:
THE SECOND HALF OF LIFE

When the new clients started coming in, I was delighted, but a little surprised. After I published the first edition of "Repurpose Your Career: A Practical Guide for Baby Boomers," I got calls and emails from a lot of Baby Boomers. They recognized themselves in my description of people who had lost their retirements in the crash.

They, too, would have to work much longer than they had anticipated, and they couldn't, or didn't want to, go back to the industry or the jobs they'd already devoted 30 years to.

Those weren't the surprise clients. They were the ones I'd expected.

But then other people, people in their 30s or 40s, started contacting me, and their stories were a little different. Many of them had put off marriage until they got their careers going, but now found themselves single, childless and disenchanted with the careers they'd made the center of their lives. Others had chosen careers that technology disrupted almost overnight, and now their skills were nearly obsolete. Many had put in a decade or more and realized their careers weren't connected st all with who they really were. They'd chosen their career because it seemed lucrative, or because someone talked them into it, or because it seemed an easy path to success. And now they just couldn't muster up another drop of enthusiasm for it.

Since my first book came out, the economic climate has changed. The technological climate continues to change. And today it's not just about Baby Boomers.

WHAT GOT ME HERE WON'T GET ME THERE ...

Rapid evolution in technology and culture has left a lot of people feeling like the foundations on which they built their expectations and decisions have shifted or disappeared altogether. Combine a shaky foundation with the promise of more change on the horizon and it's difficult to know how to confidently make choices to carry you into the next stage of your life. Among the shifts that are impacting people's lives:

- More and more work is being done by robots. Gartner predicts that by 2025, a third of jobs will have been taken over by robots, smart machines or software.

- Marriage and living in family settings is being replaced by living alone. Research by Brigham Young University shows that more people are living alone than ever. Loneliness and social isolation pose a health risk as significant as smoking and obesity.

- Social media that can help people feel connected can also lead to a greater sense of isolation, failure and depression. Studies show that people who passively engage with sites like Facebook—just look at what others are saying rather than post themselves and have conversations—actually feel more alone and more of a sense of failure and missing out than those who actively engage or don't engage at all.

- The religious landscape, long a defining cultural force, is changing. For example, from 2007 to 2014, 6 percent more people identified themselves as unaffiliated with any religion. At the same time, the number of people identifying themselves as Christians in the U.S. dropped 8 percent, according to a Pew Research Foundation report.

- A Conference Board report shows only about 48 percent of people are satisfied with their jobs, compared with 61 percent in 1987.

- Gallup reports that only about 30 percent of employees are engaged with their jobs while 50 percent are disengaged—always on the

- lookout for another job, for example. And 17 percent are actively disengaged, meaning sabotaging the efforts of other people in the organization.

This is just a sample, of course, but it demonstrates a number of fronts where things are changing. Regardless of where you stand on any of these shifts, the fact is, any change can make people feel somewhat lost and uncertain of the future. But since each generation was raised with a different ethos, these shifts impact them differently.

GENX: SUCCESSFUL CAREER = GOOD LIFE

Generation X, those people born between 1965 and 1980, often came from divorced families. These were the latchkey kids who essentially raised themselves.

Many of them grew up with the idea that happiness comes from putting your head down and getting to work. They believed that when they were successful, they would be happy. Afraid of replicating their parents' broken marriages, they delayed marriage and family until they hit that magical benchmark.

And for some, it never came.

Others reached their financial goals, looked around and asked: "Is this all there is? I thought it would be better, be more." They're not the new kids on the block anymore; in fact, the first batches started turning 50 recently. However cutting edge they were when they entered the workforce, their level of comfort with tech is likely far behind the Millennials in the workforce now. Gen Xers also see the Millennials choosing careers they can get passionate about, embracing entrepreneurship and eschewing material possessions in favor of experiences. So they wonder: "Should I take that route? Is it too late?"

One great example is a Gen X client, a financial analyst who never married and has been saving money like crazy for decades. She took a sabbatical in Southeast Asia for six weeks and it transformed her life. "These people have no money," she thought. "They're living in homes with dirt floors. But they're happy." She had pushed herself to the top of the mountain where she had been told happiness was — only to find it wasn't there.

Then she came to me.

Whether someone is alone in this place or has a partner or family, it's challenging. Historically, these are a person's top earning years, but that's not necessarily so anymore. If someone has a family, with young kids, making a Career Pivot at this point can threaten their financial security, which doesn't always go over real well. If they don't have a family, seeking a partner while you're drifting about looking for a direction feels like a recipe for disaster. Just realizing that money doesn't buy happiness doesn't tell you where to look for it next. And Gen Xers still need to make a living.

BABY BOOMERS: SHOULDN'T I BE ON A BEACH SOMEWHERE?

Then there are people in their late 50s, 60s and 70s. News reports from recent years show that Boomers, who used to envision themselves sliding comfortably into retirement, possibly on a private island, are instead committing suicide at twice the rate they used to. They feel like the world has changed so much they can't find how they fit in it anymore. They can't afford to retire, and really, they don't want to. But no one wants to hire them, partly because of the perception that they're unwilling to adapt.

Before I take this argument too far, let me express that many Baby Boomers have no intention of committing suicide, are perfectly willing to change and adapt, and are, in fact, early adopters. I'm one. But in many respects, we just operate and think differently from many Millennials. And it takes a lot of effort on both parts to make the workplace work. Millennials, who are all about diversity, have to include older people, as well as those of different faiths and gender preferences in their palettes. And Boomers have to accept the way workplaces are now.

The rules they learned about how to work — build a strategy and business plan, wait to adopt a new technology until you see if it takes off, take your place in the hierarchy — simply don't apply anymore. Nobody makes a long-term strategy

6

because things change too fast. New technology isn't a long-term investment but a stepping-stone to the next new technology. And hierarchies are getting flatter and flatter. Groups make decisions. Crowd sourcing and inclusion have replaced formal structures. For Baby Boomers who hoped to put in their time and skate out before the workplace became unrecognizable, well ... tough break. For Boomers, choosing a new direction includes preparing to rearrange their ideas about what a workplace should be while also bringing forward valuable lessons they've learned from their own careers that are still applicable. Like my client who has worked for a major cell phone carrier for nearly 30 years and sees that the path he's been treading toward success no longer exists. In a matter of years, his job will be done by robots or software and he had no backup plan.

So how do all these people begin thinking about transitioning their careers for happiness? The hurdles may be different, but the methodology is the same.

MAKE WAY FOR ROBOTS

Anyone considering a career change right now has to have a forward-looking perspective. Where are things going? What tasks can be easily done by robots, software and other technologies, and which ones require a distinctly human touch of empathy and creativity? The fact is, a lot of jobs are no longer for humans. We've all watched the robots take over manufacturing; service and creative jobs are next. Airport kiosks can check you in and issue you a boarding pass — and even verify your credentials before you get on the plane. Store checkers are being replaced by self-check stations. Some hotels have robots bring you your extra towels, and robot journalists are now being employed to write stories and commercial content. Nearly everything you want done can be done by self-service, and many Generation X and Millennials prefer it that way.

They'd rather buy an item online than do the song and dance with a salesperson. For that matter, many would rather pay to ride in a car that drives itself than buy their own vehicles. Whatever industry you're in or are interested in, it's wise to look at what future is predicted in terms of job apportionment for humans and for robots. We have to capitalize on what makes us human, and that includes our relationships.

WHO YOU KNOW

After years of helping people pivot their careers I can say this with complete confidence: Your social and professional networks are the most important piece of any career change. Who do you know in the industry you're interested in? Who do you know at the company where you want to work? Who do you know who has connections with these kinds of people? A number of companies, including

LinkedIn and Facebook's professional pages, have been built to capitalize on the power of human networks.

In 1973, sociologist Mark Granovetter wrote a paper called "The Strength of Weak Ties." He argued that, in some ways, connections between people who don't know one another well might be more powerful than those among close friends or family. The reason is that when you know someone well, you know their weaknesses, tendencies and inclinations and can weigh their opinion through that lens. But if several people you don't know well recommend a book, a movie or a course of action you are more likely to be influenced by that. People still study Granovetter's theory because it has become more and more important in this age of social media. Your ties to people in your network, even those who are not close to you, may have more impact on your future than you can imagine. For example, many of us have people we knew 20 years ago who think well of us and who have landed in completely new industries with entirely new networks that we could tap into. But we rarely think of them when we're looking for a new opportunity. Those are precisely the kinds of weak ties Granovetter was talking about.

No one makes a change without help. It takes connections, supporters, a tribe to help you transition from one place to the next. And one benefit to the changing world is access to information about who might be members of that tribe.

KNOW THYSELF

You, of course, are the most important person to know. Do you even know what your talents are? What makes you love one job and not another? Do you know how to describe the kinds of environments that put you "in the zone" from a work perspective?

People tend to look at jobs simply in terms of salary and benefits but there are so many other things that matter. Like your commute, and what the office is like.

For many people, the focus isn't on what they do, but who their teams are. As long as they connect to the people around them, they can be happy in any job.

Other people need a certain level of stasis or change. I had a client who realized that one of her biggest drawbacks was that she would rapidly become unhappy in a job. This caused a lot of problems when she was hired to do one thing and, six months or a year later, she was still doing it and hating it more and more. We realized she needed a lot of variety and change. She was happy figuring out how to solve a problem and training others how to do the work that needed doing to keep the organizational machinery running, but then she needed a new challenge. Making that part of her job search and negotiations was the key to finding a position that worked for her.

Another client loved cleaning up messes. If some department was a catastrophe, some process outdated, some management system dysfunctional, he would go in and find solutions, clean it up and get it all running smoothly. But after that, he was bored. He needed a career where cleaning up messes was his job.

No matter how lucrative, high-status or secure a job may be, if it doesn't fit who you are, it will be a gilded cage. You have to find the work that fulfills you as an individual while earning you enough to live according to your own standards. That requires a process.

There are a lot of moving parts, a lot of mental, emotional and lifestyle shifts, and a lot of decisions about what's really MOST important to your happiness and success.

Making a change isn't an overnight task. You took time to get yourself where you are and perfect your current way of thinking and operating. And it will take time to learn to think and function in a different way. It will take time to understand yourself and to cultivate the skills needed to pivot to the work that suits you best. It's worth it.

ACTION STEPS:

- ✓ Are you successful in your career but still not happy? Reflect on how you got to this point.

- ✓ Assess whether your job could be replaced by a robot.

- ✓ Have you had weak ties assist you in your career? Reflect on when and where. We will use this later.

For additional resources, check out:

Repurpose Your Career Resource Center
https://careerpivot.com/RYC-Resources

YOUR FIRST STEPS TOWARD YOUR NEW LIFE

I was on my way to China, standing in line waiting to board the plane, when the question that had been picking at the back of my mind sprung up in front of me, huge and fully formed: What are you DOING?

Less than a year before, I had survived a nearly fatal bicycle accident. My bike hit the car—head on. Our combined speeds were 50 miles an hour. The car was totaled, and I should have been. But miraculously, though I spent five days in a trauma center, I recovered fully. At those speeds, there is a 10 percent chance of survival.

I was alive. The one life I get, that I know of. And I was once again getting on a plane to go somewhere I didn't care to go to teach people how to design leading edge routers and switches that wouldn't change the world. What was I doing with my life?

I did take that trip and several others after it. (Sorry — there's no dramatic running-off-the-tarmac scene.) But that moment launched me on a journey to create a life I believed in. It took years, painful mistakes and several course corrections. In fact, I don't think I'll ever be done learning and changing.

But one thing I discovered while trying to find a good path for my life was that I was not alone — far from it.

When I shared the steps I was taking to change my life, friends and acquaintances looked at me with an expression of skepticism that tried to mask a mixture of longing and fear. They wanted to change their lives, too. How had I done it? Was it possible for them?

REINVENTION REQUIRES STRATEGY

I am a data guy who worked over 20 years for IBM and has years of experience training and teaching. I like systems. I like finding the most efficient and effective way of doing things. And I've learned that the most realistic approach is the Career Pivot: a series of half steps that gets you to your goal.

While making my own changes, and working with others on theirs, I've developed a pretty solid system. But if it's going to succeed for you, you will need to be really honest with yourself about where you are now. For example:

- What is your skill set?

- What are your resources — both financial and personal? When you make this change, will your family be behind you? Do you have a support system?

- How is your health? This will impact what kind of career you can consider.

- What is your financial situation and what future financial needs can you anticipate?

- How do you feel about change?

- Are you ready to give this process whatever is required to get it done?

The last one is important. Picking a new direction for your life requires traveling uncomfortable new territory.

And here's another question: Are you in your right mind? I'm not asking whether you're crazy. But all of us have a positive, sage brain and a negative brain. If you're thinking in terms of running away from your job or your life, chances are you're in your negative brain. Your negative brain tends to bring a whole lot of baggage to the process that you don't need. Your negative brain tells you how ill equipped you are for what you want, how hopeless it all is, how unfriendly other people are being. It's a real downer.

My client Lisa was laid off and very upset about it. She was experiencing a lot of stress, anxiety and anger. I don't know if it's energy, pheromones or subtle clues, but when we're stressed like that, we repel people. Nobody wants to be around it. If Lisa had gone looking for a job in that state, she would likely have been really unsuccessful, which would have made things even more discouraging for her.

Instead, I taught her a technique I learned from the book "Positive Intelligence" about naming your judges. Research shows that 70 percent of our self-talk is negative. But it helps a lot to name the negative voices — your judges — who are talking to you. One person, for example, named their judge Darth Vader. Lisa named hers Stresszilla. If you recognize your judges as being intruders on your thought process instead of part of your thought process, it helps you to turn them off.

Instead of looking for a job right away, Lisa took a several months to nurture herself and recover from the shock. Then when she was ready to apply, everything from her interview answers to her body language communicated a much healthier message.

But you also need to ascertain whether you're running away from something or running to something. This book will help you figure that out. If you're running away from something, you need to reframe your thinking so that you're running toward something. If you don't, it's a pretty safe bet you'll wind up in a mess very similar to the one you're currently trying to escape. For example, instead of trying to escape your controlling boss, look for a company with a management system that's big on autonomy and empowerment. Instead of trying to get out of a corporate environment, seek a job with more community, team spirit and a more close-knit team.

For this journey, you will need to embark on a lot of introspection: Who are you? How did you get here? Without this step, you might as well not bother, because you're likely to pedal hard to wind up in the same position you're in now.

You will have to stop being the expert with 20 years' experience and become the novice, asking for help. You may have to take courses, become smart about social media sites like LinkedIn and adjust your idea of what "the good life" is. If any of that sounds like a deal breaker, this may not be the moment for you to take the plunge.

But if it is the moment, I've got the tools to help you on your Career Pivot. Read on.

ACTION STEPS:

- ✓ Will your family and friends support you in making a pivot? Go ask them!

- ✓ What barriers have prevented you from making career pivots? Write down what you need to address them.

- ✓ Why now? Identify what has motivated you to read this book and take the first step in making a career pivot.

For additional resources, check out:

Repurpose Your Career Resource Center
https://careerpivot.com/RYC-Resources

WHEN THE CLOUDS PART: MOMENTS OF CLARITY

Sam was in his late 50s in 2014, when he got laid off for the second time in five years. He'd been fanatical about saving for retirement. And here he was again, on the hunt for a job. It was fall. There was little use in job hunting during the holidays. So he went on a walkabout.

A walkabout is a ritual practiced by aboriginal tribes of Australia. They send 13-year-old boys out into the wilderness to follow the trails their ancestors took. It's a rite of passage to see if they can survive on their own. Sam's walkabout was a little different. He got a rail pass and decided to head west and see the country.

He slept on friends' couches. He slept in his car. Once he even spent the night, illegally, on a park bench. He was gone for a month. And while he was away, he had an epiphany. He'd always been worried about having enough money for the lifestyle he expected to live in retirement. But now he didn't feel like he needed it. All he really needed was good food, good coffee, a place to sleep and a place to work out.

This was Sam's moment of clarity.

Moments of clarity are those times when the assorted junk that plagues your mind— your annoying co-worker, your extra 15 pounds, the ugly tile in your bathroom or your battle over which one of you gets a new car—suddenly vanishes in the face of something life-altering. It might be that your child is sick, or your spouse or you. It might be a death in the family, a divorce, a layoff or a natural disaster. It might even be good news, like an inheritance or an opportunity.

Or a walkabout.

Whatever it is, it turns your perspective upside down. Suddenly the way you were living doesn't make sense. "Why did I ever think that ugly tile was important?" you think to yourself. "Why did I spend so many sleepless nights over that argument? Why didn't I pursue my dreams? How did I not see the truth before?"

A moment of clarity may or may not touch on your career. But if it does, it reveals truths you've been ignoring or deliberately hiding from yourself.

You might realize that your parents pushed you into a career you didn't want, or that the company you work for has institutional barriers that will never let you succeed.

You might see that you always wind up with narcissistic bosses and wonder what that is about. Or you might realize you habitually undermine

20

yourself, selling yourself short to more powerful colleagues.

Because of a dramatic — if temporary — change in circumstances, nothing looks the same as it did yesterday. The filters that prevented you from seeing things as they are have come down and you have an opportunity to learn something about yourself.

You learn what is really important to you at those times.

The problem is, those filters go back up quickly. The moment passes, and, next thing you know, the bathroom tile is bugging you again. If you don't act in that moment of clarity, or set a change in place, you'll go on as you were with a nagging sense of missed opportunity.

I am happy to say I can see many times I acted in a moment of clarity and was always better for it.

For example:

MY OWN WALKABOUT: When I was in my 20s, working for IBM, I took two weeks' vacation and two weeks without pay. I went to Colorado, Utah and Arizona to the Grand Canyon. It took me a few days to begin decompressing and realize how stressed I was. It took more days until I got to the point where I couldn't remember what day it was. By the time I came back, having spent only $500, I realized I could live on a lot less money. I also was a changed person. That was when I met my wife,

Lotus. If I had been the anxious wreck I was when I left, I don't know that it ever would have become the 30-year marriage we've enjoyed.

THE DAY MY SON WAS BORN: The following year was amazing and I made a lot of personal changes during that time.

WHEN I GOT HURT: In December 1992, I ruptured the L4/L5 discs in my lower back. I either had to get an operation or take three months off on disability to recover. I chose to take the time off. I'd always overloaded myself with projects, but now I was forced to relax.

In the process, I discovered peace. All my previous stress seemed so unnecessary in light of this revelation of being calm. Simple things became delightful. When I went back to work at IBM, the company was near bankruptcy and my stressed-out colleagues were panicked about being unable to afford their bloated lifestyles. But I saw clearly that I didn't want to swap my newfound peace for this anxiety again. I was willing to make whatever changes necessary to my career and lifestyle to preserve my contentment.

MY BICYCLE ACCIDENT: It left me wondering why I was placed on this Earth. I then planned my career pivot to teaching high school math.

The thing is, whatever you learned in that moment of clarity is still in you, somewhere, though it no longer takes a front seat in your awareness. And it still has things to teach you.

So when I work with clients, I always have them go back and look for moments of clarity in their lives. I have them chronicle each one and what it taught them.

Then, because these moments might not be as dramatically clear in a career situation, I have them go back and chronicle information about every job they've ever held.

You'd be amazed at the patterns that emerge. Try this. Fill out your own job history using these criteria.

START OF JOB

Description: Briefly summarize the job and its duties. Reason You Took This Job:

Influenced By: Who or what influenced you to take this job? How You Found This Job: Colleague? Online site? Headhunter? Environment: What was the environment of this place?

Feel: How did the environment make you feel?

Team or Solo: Were you part of a team or were you on your own? What was your role? Were you the team leader or a participant? How well did the team function? Did you like being on this team?

Independence: Were you free to control how you did your job, or were the rules created for you?

Manager's Style: What was the management style of your supervisor?

Work Pace/Schedule: Did you have control of your schedule? How varied were your activities during the course of a day? How much physical activity did this job require?

Rewards: Did you feel valued? If so, what actions by your employer demonstrated to you that your contribution was valued?

Best Thing About This Job:

Worst Thing About This Job:

What You Learned About What You Need:

What You Learned About What You Do Not Need:

END OF JOB

Reason You Left This Job:

Who or What Influenced You to Leave:

Exit Status: Did you have another job to go to when you left?

If you do this for every position or job you have ever had and put them in order, you will see a pattern. Most of us have made the same mistakes in our careers more than once. I call this Career Insanity: doing the same thing over and over but expecting a different outcome each time.

In Sam's case, he realized that his spouse may not be as tickled about selling everything and becoming a vagabond as he is. They have a big house in Connecticut and upper middle-class lifestyle. He's decided to look for another job and give them a couple of years to figure out what kind of a life they want going forward.

Moments of clarity are moments when your perception shifts. You're likely to have one after reflecting back on your life and your career. You're likely to see patterns and missed opportunities that have brought you to where you are now.

Take this as a moment of clarity. What do you want to do from today on?

ACTION STEPS:

- ✓ Retrace moments in your life when you suddenly saw life differently. These could be because of a problem, like an illness or layoff, or something good, like marriage or the birth of a child.

- ✓ Write down what you learned in those moments, whether you followed the lessons they taught or ignored them, and what the results were.

- ✓ Retrace your job history. What did you learn about yourself and your needs from each of the jobs you've held?

For additional resources, check out:

Repurpose Your Career Resource Center
https://careerpivot.com/RYC-Resources/

TO GET WHAT YOU NEED, YOU MUST KNOW WHAT YOU NEED

To paraphrase Lewis Carroll, "If you don't know where you're going, any road will get you there." But if you're tired of wandering around, never arriving at your goal, you need to figure out where you really want to be.

What do you actually need and want out of life and what role does your job play in that? This is a much bigger question than most people think. It's not just about pay, perks or a nice boss. Many of us have a host of underlying needs we never recognize. In fact, people are often really surprised by what assessments reveal about their deepest needs. Then, after a moment of reflection, the light goes on: "Oh, THAT's what that is! I never had a name for it before.

One woman I worked with, who thought she was immune to status, learned she REALLY valued aligning herself with key decision-makers and knowing who was in charge of every project. When that didn't work out, she felt frustrated but she couldn't say why.

Many people really need to be in charge of their own schedules and organizational systems. If they can't, they're constantly frustrated.

Not getting what you need isn't always as obvious as having an abusive boss or unsanitary working conditions, but it can create low-grade anxiety and frustration all day, every day, that builds up.

You can transform your work life by seeking what you really need from the job—whether that's within your current occupation or in a new one. But you have to figure out what that is and learn how to ask for it.

REWARDS

One of the top reasons we change jobs is because we do not feel valued. Most people want and need some kind of reward for doing good work. This can come in many forms:

- The right mission
- Bonus or financial reward
- Public recognition or an award
- Pat on the back and thanks from management
- Pat on the back and thanks from your peers
- Pat on the back and thanks from your customer

For me, the best reward is a pat on the back from my customer. After my epiphany with my bicycle accident, I became a high school math teacher. There, my customers were my students.

In case you haven't heard, students outside of Afterschool Specials and Hallmark ads rarely thank their teachers. But in my second year, my previous year's students did come back and thank me for taking extra time with them, communicating in a way that was relevant to them and redefining rules to help them succeed.

That first year, working long days without ever getting the reward that met my needs was torture. I didn't understand my needs at the time, so I couldn't put a finger on what was making life so stressful. In an urban school, on a new job, there are plenty of places to assign stress. Had I known what was really getting to me, I could have worked on coping mechanisms that would have helped a lot.

I have a client who got more and more depressed because his boss never told him he was doing a good job. Because he's the kind of person who tells people, verbally, when they're doing well, he has an expectation that if he's doing well someone will tell him. And if they don't, he fears it means he's screwing up, in danger of getting fired or at the very least not thought of highly. Regardless of other signs he was excelling, the fact that his boss didn't say anything constantly tugged at him. So I told him to tell his boss, which he was reluctant to do. But finally he walked into his boss's office and said, "So

I was just wondering. You never really say much about my performance. How'm I doing?"

"Great!" his boss replied enthusiastically. "We're really pleased with your work."

"Oh," my client replied. "Would you mind telling me from time to time? It's very helpful."

His boss responded "Sure." And then he looked at my client earnestly and said: "Thank you for telling me."

Most managers want to know how to manage better and they can't really figure out all their different employees' feedback styles.

Some people never care about verbal feedback, but they do expect raises and bonuses. Others are most concerned about the reward of being recognized as a valuable team member and wind up not pushing for higher financial compensation. This can lead to pay inequity.

I had a client whose boss never gave raises. But he gave bonuses. That was the boss's preferred method of handling money. It was not my client's. He was looking for the security of an increased paycheck.

Some people are best rewarded by time off, more time for themselves. Others crave more challenging projects, the chance to learn new skills.

I find that for those in the nonprofit world or in the military the most important reward is working on a mission that resonates with them.

What kind of reward system have you been accustomed to and how did it suit you? Was there a reward you wish you'd received more of?

FREEDOM

Freedom is … the ability to take a two-hour client lunch without explaining it to anybody, go to a doctor's appointment without a big hassle, take Friday afternoon off and make it up Saturday morning. Or it can be the freedom to use your imagination in creating products and solutions. Or the freedom to wear jeans on the job, work from home or to speak your mind without multi-layered corporate censure. Really, freedom can be defined many ways. Most of those definitions fall roughly into three areas:

- Freedom from micromanagement: supervisors constantly telling you how to do your job

- Being creative and individualistic in your approach

- The level of structure and rules and who gets to create them.

- I work with a lot of very experienced professionals who need all three kinds of freedom. They want to do the job and for everyone else to get out of the way. As long as their results meet or exceed expectations, they don't want to answer to anyone.

Freedom is increasingly important to employees. Several new approaches to management with flatter hierarchies make it possible for employees at all levels to essentially design their own jobs as long as the work gets done.

If you could create your own job description in terms of freedom, what would it include?

RESPECT AND EMOTIONAL SUPPORT

When we go to work, we expect our peers to treat us in a way that makes us feel that we belong.

Some of us prefer a culture where others talk to us very directly, with minimal emotion: "Just give me the facts." That communicates respect for our position.

Other people hate that way of communicating. They want their feelings and perceptions to be included in the conversation. Most people fall somewhere in between. How do we select jobs and environments where we will get the respect and emotional support we want and need?

Through Strategic Networking, which we'll talk about in a later chapter, you can explore different environments to assess the directness in communication and the emotional support provided. You could ask someone who works at a company you're interested in about his or her supervisor's communication style. Even if the person has a problem with the supervisor and is being careful about expressing it, you can usually read between the lines. Look for keywords. If people talk about a "direct, no-nonsense, efficient and professional" style, you can figure that's what they seek in a candidate. If the sound of that relaxes you, you might be a good fit. If, on the other hand, someone talks about a "warm, supportive, relational" workplace, you can bet that emotions are welcome there.

VARIETY

Do you like to multitask at work? One of the key happiness factors at work is how much variety you are afforded. I have many clients who NEED lots of variety and love to multitask. I, on the other hand, like steady work to do with very few interruptions.

My client Sally was a communication expert who needed lots of variety. So when she got a job at a chamber of commerce with fewer than 50 employees, she was in heaven. They had her doing email marketing, writing press releases, doing social media. ... She might have five kinds of tasks in a day. It was wonderful. Then they started hiring more people and her job became much more specialized. Now she did the same few tasks over and over and she was bored. She had learned some key things about herself in the chamber of commerce job: she loves variety and she's easily distracted. She works best by herself, in her own office, on a multitude of tasks.

So she started looking for a new job that fit that description. But then an unexpected opportunity caught her eye. A large company wanted her to manage a staff of 12 people. It would not have much variety. She'd be working in an open office with others instead of in her own private office.

She'd never considered a job like that and she was flattered that they trusted her to manage 12 people. So she was thinking about taking the job, even though it had none of the things she was looking for.

"Do you want to manage 12 people?" I asked her.

Her face kind of fell. No. Not really. The idea was attractive. But she knew when it came down to how she liked to work, she much preferred working on her own.

"Could you handle an open office?" I pressed. Another "no."

Taking a job because of the idea of it is a lot like moving in with someone because it seems like it might be fun. By the time you figure out you actually hate the reality, you're in for a painful process to get out of it. Sally needed to focus her search on smaller companies that needed fewer people who could wear a lot more hats.

Another client of mine, Rick, is a structured anarchist. You would never know it to look at him. Every time I've seen him, every hair is in place. His clothes are impeccable. He is the former CFO of some major nonprofits, with an MBA in finance, and comes across as the most orderly person you could ever meet. I did his Birkman profile—a behavior and personality assessment I have all my clients do—and it shows that structure is really important to him.

But Rick doesn't particularly care for walking into a situation that's already orderly. He prefers to impose his own order on things. He loves to walk into a situation that's in chaos and clean it up. Once it's cleaned up and running smoothly, he's bored.

He's been hired to come in and straighten out messes before, but it never dawned on any of his previous employers that once one problem was solved, it would behoove them, and make Rick extremely happy, to find him a new mess. So he would get a new job, clean up the chaos and then begin to get frustrated and eventually quit and go looking again. When we looked at his previous jobs — why he took each one, why he left—a pattern began to emerge.

Rick, it turned out, is a "firefighter," someone who loves to stop a mundane course of work in order to "put out a fire." People in the financial world don't have a lot of firefighters because if your financial situation is a mess, that alarms investors, stockholders and customers. But in the engineering world, where I'm from, fighting fires is normal. I had client who came out of IBM and got a job as director of software for another company. They'd put her on a problem project, she'd fix it and then they'd move her to the next problem. She loved her job.

Rick was working for an employer who realized they were having some trouble with their channel partners. His boss was planning to do a survey to identify the issues. Rick stepped in. "No, wait," he said. "First, let me interview the top 10 channel partners. From that interview, I'll create a survey to identify the top 25 issues and actions we can take to resolve them."

Rick's process revealed specific problems and helped him form a list of actions they could take, from training to communication, to improve the company significantly. The information about what Rick had done went all the way up to the CEO, who said: "You're the only person who could have figured this out. We've been trying to solve these problems for 10 years!"

Then Rick knew what he wanted. He wanted to keep solving hard problems, wherever they cropped up in the company. It took Rick and the company a year to figure out where he belonged. But once they did, he couldn't have been happier.

Are you a person who wants a lot of variety? Do you get distracted easily? Do you get bored easily? Here are a few questions to ask yourself:

- Are you more or less productive when you have lots of things going on simultaneously? Many people instinctively say more. But are you sure?

- At what point does multitasking become stressful? Is it when you have three things going on at the same time? Five? Ten?

- What happens when you are interrupted frequently? Do you become stressed?

When I was teaching high school, my day was pretty regimented. I was doing the same thing all day. In my second year of teaching, I had five sections of Algebra II, which meant I taught the same lesson five times. This would drive some people crazy, but it fit well with my personality. My schedule was decided for me down to the minute. And that was OK, because I got to be on my feet all day.

Again, that would drive some people crazy. But I can't sit at a desk for more than 45 minutes at a time. I loved that I was on my feet and moving all day.

Think about what the perfect culture would be for you based on positive experiences and relationships you've had either at work, on teams or personally. These give you some good insights as to what your needs are. Then you have to learn to ask for them.

ACTION STEPS:

✓ Reflect back to the job or position that made you feel most rewarded. What did you receive that made you feel good?

✓ Write down what you need from a job, including such intangibles as freedom, respect, physical activity and variety.

✓ Write down the kind of culture you prefer to work in: small or large company, institutional or entrepreneurial, etc.

✓ Download the Career Reflection worksheet from the Repurpose Your Career Resource Center.

For additional resources, check out:

Repurpose Your Career Resource Center
https://careerpivot.com/RYC-Resources/

WHAT IS YOUR PERSONAL OPERATING SYSTEM?

Most of my clients have a whole system of needs, stressors and behaviors they are only marginally aware of. These things are constantly humming in the background, like the operating system of a computer. We don't think about them, but they impact everything about the way we feel and function.

One person might be extremely deliberate about making decisions. He researches every car on the market before buying one. He weighs every variable, constantly looking for opportunities or pitfalls others miss. It's how he's always been. Trying to make a decision faster makes him anxious. He worries about making mistakes that could have dire consequences.

At work, he gets frustrated with his boss, who seems to expect him to do hours of research to prepare for questions she might throw at him at meetings. She wants input and decisions on issues he couldn't possibly have had time to weigh carefully.

In truth, she doesn't expect hours of research. She makes decisions quickly on the facts at hand and expects him to do the same. Such a thing would never dawn on him. It's too crazy, capricious, stressful.

He doesn't realize he needs a job where his thoroughness would be an asset. He just thinks he needs to get away from her.

That's where assessments come in so handy.

FIRST STEP TO CAREER BLISS: KNOW THYSELF

Many of us go after jobs thinking things like this: "I want to get away from my boss. I want more money. I want to work for a bigger organization, or a smaller one." We think we've isolated the problem with our last job or career, so we set out to solve the problem we identified.

But frequently, all we've really done is isolate a symptom, not the problem itself.

To find a career that will satisfy you in the long run, you need to understand many things about yourself: what you need, what stresses you and what makes you happy. Assessments reveal truths about us that we might not even realize affect our careers. They can be the first step to understanding yourself, which is the first step to pursuing your own happiness and satisfaction.

I have done a bunch of assessments: MBTI (Myers-Briggs), DiSC, Kolbe, StrengthsFinder 2.0 and

Birkman. For me, the most valuable for gaining insight into my own needs was the Birkman.

When I took it, several years ago, I learned that I need plenty of alone time. I had no idea. I knew that, as a younger man, I'd been alone more than I liked. And I knew that I didn't enjoy my first job at IBM alone in a cubicle. I can also tell you I am quite social, I love to work a crowd and go to many gatherings every week. (In Austin, where I live, you could attend about a thousand a week if you had the time and stamina). What I didn't realize until I took the Birkman was that it's not an either/or. I didn't like being alone all the time. Nor could I just leap into constant social activity. I need a good balance of both.

That's a piece of information that could save me from many dissatisfying job changes. Without it, I could think: "I HATE being alone in my cubicle all day. I need a job where I'm working with people!" Then I go after a job to solve my isolation problem and wind up in meetings, client calls or networking events from morning till night, exhausted and longing for my monastic cubicle.

That's the kind of thing the Birkman reveals. The Birkman is 298 fairly repetitious questions that ask what you do, think and believe and what you think "most people" do, think and believe?

For example, "Do you think it's more important to be honest than to avoid hurting people's feelings?

Do you think others feel honesty is more important that protecting people's feelings?"

It's a strange test that, after you've been asked the same question about four different ways, can make you think: "Who knows? Who cares? Why are you asking this again?"

But then you sit down with a Birkman advisor who explains what your answers say about you. And suddenly it's like you're with a psychic who is telling you things that maybe you didn't want to know. But, to be honest, you sort of knew them, deep down.

I had a client who landed in the wrong career because of things he didn't know about himself. In high school, he scored really high on the math portion of his PSAT. "Get thee to an engineering school," a counselor told him. So he did.

Here's what the counselor wasn't aware of: This guy is a very empathetic, emotional person. Most engineers are very low on the empathy scale. Over the years, he learned to act like his colleagues, but he was miserable. The Birkman confirmed that empathy wasn't a weakness in his work social skills, it was a strength he had to hide because of the environments he'd chosen. Now he could look for a career where both his engineering skills and his empathy would prove valuable.

ADJUSTING FOR YOUR POS

There was a great article in Fortune Magazine on the value of the Birkman called "Are You a Good Fit for Your Job?"

Senior Editor Jennifer Reingold learned — among other things — that while she's keen on taking the direct approach with others, she's not too thrilled when she's on the receiving end.

As it turns out, that's true for a lot of salespeople, too. Salespeople have to sit back and listen at first until they gain the confidence of their prospect, then lean in and start to push. This may have nothing to do with their personalities. Either the listening or the pushing might be totally opposed to how they are naturally. They have to learn to do it because that's the dynamic of sales. But frequently they don't like being a recipient of the very same treatment.

A lot of us learn to behave in ways that aren't natural for us for the sake of our jobs. Sometimes that makes us miserable. Other times we just need to learn some important coping skills.

For example, when I do speaking engagements, I usually do a lot of networking before and after my talk. So when I stand up in front of all those people and say: "I am an introvert," it always gets a laugh.

But I *am* an introvert.

I can schmooze and socialize with the best of them, but I had to learn how to do it and ultimately, it exhausts me. I enjoy being around people. But that's not where I get my energy. I get my energy from time alone. And that is the definition of an introvert.

Our society it is biased toward extroverts. Extroverts make more money. They're taken more seriously as leaders. They're perceived as more competent even though, as Susan Cain pointed out in her book "Quiet: The Power of Introverts In a World That Can't Stop Talking," many of our great thinkers and artists have been introverts.

Cain tells a story of an exercise at Harvard Business School in which a class formed two teams. The professor told the teams they were on a plane that has crashed in the Alaskan wilderness and that they must identify what to take with them to survive. One team member actually grew up in Alaska and had spent time in the wilderness. He knew exactly what to take. But he was an introvert and no one asked him. When the teams reported back, the professor learned that they had a native Alaskan but that he had not weighed in on what to bring. When he asked why, the team leader said: "He never spoke up."

Cain's point was that the world is missing out by not listening to introverts. But there's another point here, too: If you're an introvert, you need to find a way to cope so that you don't become the one who is missing out. Cain, herself an introvert who pretended to be an extrovert, suggests that introverts, if they're going to be around people, need little restorative niches during the day to do something they enjoy.

I had a client who loved to knit. I recommended that she take a few moments between some of her back-to-back meetings to knit. Another client had to present six times at a conference. We decided he should take breaks in between, go back to his room and read a book. For another client, the break was to take pictures—just that little act of observing distanced her some from the crowd.

I had one client who was a top-level sales rep married to another top-level sales rep. They both acted like extroverts, but she was a closet introvert. So at a conference when everybody else was gearing up to go out to dinner, he was ready to join them. She, on the other hand, was done. She couldn't handle one more social interaction. So she would head back to the hotel room and order room service. He would tell everyone she wasn't feeling well — because, in their world, that's better than being an introvert.

There are actually a lot of us introverts out there in extrovert clothing. We can act extroverted a lot more easily, and become much more resilient when it comes to social situations, if we make an adjustment and gives ourselves breaks.

GETTING THE RIGHT PROGRAM FOR YOUR POS

In fact, a giant factor in being happy in your career is figuring out what makes your personal operating system work best.

Many of the women I work with (and, in fact, many women I talk to) are "stealth competitors." They were raised to believe that if they worked hard, people would recognize their contribution and reward them. Their peers would characterize these women as very "sweet." They are affable, get along well with others, never hog the limelight. They just seem content to do their jobs. If asked, that's how they might describe themselves.

But the Birkman often shows that these women are frustrated and angry. They don't understand why they're not getting recognition, praise and raises. The signals they're sending out—what the Birkman calls their "effective behavior"—communicate that they are perfectly fine without the kinds of rewards other people receive. They may, in fact, have been hired because they seemed like they would ask very little. And that's what they get. When they see those results, my clients always look shocked. "That's true!" they exclaim.

These women often don't realize that they are holding their bosses or clients accountable to give recognition and rewards that they've never asked for or even seemed to need. This could really hurt their work relationships if they don't understand

and adjust for it. But the Birkman spells all of that out, and a Birkman advisor would explain that these women need to ask for what they want. That's not always easy, as we'll talk about later. But it's crucial for their happiness.

A lot of men and women succeed in their fields because they are highly organized. They can easily prioritize tasks and focus their attention and energy where it will be most effective in that moment. These people aren't at all intimidated by having a lot to do, as long as they get to decide how to do it. But give a person like that a boss who is trying to "help" by writing out a detailed list of tasks and you will have one stressed-out employee. The boss has just hobbled his best racehorse. The Birkman often shows these highly organized people that they must insist on a position where the culture or the boss will allow them to say: "Point me toward the goal and get out of my way." Then, watch 'em go!

If, on the other hand, you're someone who feels uncomfortable with a lot of autonomy and prefers to have your boss's and your company's expectations clearly spelled out so you don't have to make a lot of decisions, the boss with the detailed list would be ideal.

Some people function beautifully with a lot of distractions. They might like listening to music while they work, welcome co-workers dropping by with questions, and switch easily from one quick task to the next.

47

Other people, me included, need stretches of uninterrupted work time to accomplish our best results. Being interrupted all the time shatters our thoughts and leaves us almost too frustrated to get anything done. Some people may not even realize that that's something they need to consider when looking at a job or career change. Is this a position where you could focus intensely for several hours or are you likely to be interrupted by customers or colleagues?

Spend time considering how you work best. It can make all the difference in the world in terms of job satisfaction and performance.

In July of 2010, I went on a grueling trip to Australia to teach a four-day sales class. At the end of each day, some of the Aussie salespeople wanted to take me out for drinks. It would have been fun, but I knew I had to say no. I had a quiet dinner with a few close friends and went back to my room to watch the Tour de France. Like my sales-rep client, I knew this was what I had to do to properly take care of myself.

There are a number of remarkable things my clients have discovered from the Birkman. One woman found she was much happier in her job when she had a desk by the window and could bring plants to her work area.

Another client discovered that it really upset her when someone with less expertise stepped in on decisions about her part of a project. After taking her assessment and learning the results, she knew she would still have to deal with that from team members or clients, but she was prepared to devise ways to handle it more gracefully.

STILL LEARNING FROM THE BIRKMAN

It took me months to internalize the information I learned about myself in the Birkman report, with the help of my advisor. I still go back, review my report and I STILL am learning about myself.

Another thing I've learned over time is that I have an unusual competency with reading the Birkman. Many of the people who do the sort of thing I do have backgrounds in social work, psychology or counseling. They rely more on their intuition and people skills. But I'm a recovering engineer and I read patterns. At this point, I can meet with someone and learn from just a few pieces of information a lot more about him. If he is a closet creative, the following things are probably true: He wants a lot of respect, is an introvert, is fairly emotional, is a stealth competitor, doesn't like order, doesn't want a boss, wants lots of variety and wants the freedom to do it his way. Of course, people surprise me and I walk in with an open mind, but the patterns generally hold.

The Birkman has also given me other tools to help people understand themselves. I worked with a client who used to work for a hedge fund but loved redecorating rooms. She thought she was a creative thinker. I could tell she wasn't. She was a linear, conceptual thinker. So I gave her a task that I give many clients: "Go find three problems you solved at work and three in your personal life. How did you solve them? What was your thought process?"

She talked about how she approached redecorating a room: "First I look at the colors, and then I look at the shapes in the room and then I look at the arrangement and then..."

I looked at her and said, "So you have a process that you follow." She said, "I do not!"

"You just described a detailed process that you follow." She looked at me in surprise.

"Oh, you are right."

I had another client who is now a UX designer. She thought of herself as a process- oriented thinker. I asked her how she found her apartment.

She looked at prices and then locations. She came up with a list of apartment buildings and looked at them one by one. But when she walked into her current place, she "just knew it was right."

She was, in fact, highly intuitive. She had some problem-solving processes that were linear, but she also used her intuition a lot more than she knew.

When you understand these things about yourself, it helps you make much better decisions that are likely to have much better outcomes. It's fun, too!

What could a Birkman or similar assessment tell you that would set you on not just a new path or a different path, but on the right path?

ACTION STEPS:

✓ Take a career assessment test, such as the Birkman, to uncover rules and motivators you didn't even know you had: your personal operating system. Contact me at careerpivot.com/contact-me to schedule an assessment.

For additional resources, check out:

Repurpose Your Career Resource Center
https://careerpivot.com/RYC-Resources/

CAREER MISTAKES:
FAILURE IS A GREAT OPTION

There's a gripping moment in the movie "Apollo 13" where Flight Director Gene Kranz (played by Ed Harris) is telling his Houston team that they have to figure out a way to bring the crew back.

"Failure is not an option!" he barks.

That's probably true if you're Mission Control for a bunch of people floating in a dead spaceship. In fact, Kranz named his autobiography "Failure Is Not an Option: Mission Control from Mercury to Apollo 13 and Beyond." That mentality is fortifying and inspiring, like Cortez burning the ships. My generation grew up with that idea, that "Never surrender. Never accept failure" credo. But the truth is, these days, it's mostly bullshit.

If you're like most people, failure is sometimes not only an option, but it's inevitable. And to take it one step further, it's essential. You don't learn unless you fail. And unless you're willing to fail, you aren't likely to venture anything very impressive. Some of my biggest leaps forward began with tripping. I can pinpoint the moments of my biggest career failures. And because I went back and analyzed them like the good recovering engineer that I am, I can see how each one propelled me forward. Here they are:

MISTAKE 1: I WAS SEDUCED BY A FORMER MANAGER

To be clear, I'm a happily married man. But in the late 1990s, when I was working for IBM in a briefing center, I was bored. My job was to give the inside scoop on various products to IBM's leading customers. For me, it was an easy job. The presentations were deeply technical, but I understood them and crafted the information into six or seven presentations that I could have given in my sleep.

The great part of the job was that, as an ambassador for our top clients, I was highly visible to upper management. For that reason, they often asked me to present at leading conferences. I got tons of swag: jackets, shirts, hats, bags...

But after seven years of doing this job, I was ready for a new challenge.

My manager (who was great) had left the previous year to work for IBM Global Services, the IBM consulting arm. She knew I was bored and worked on me to join her group. She painted a very rosy picture, so, after about six months, I made the leap. It was one of the biggest mistakes of my career.

I had allowed myself to be seduced, as did several other people she knew in the organization who had deep consulting experience. I don't think she intended anything negative for me. But I should have done my homework rather than just accepting her description of the job. I realized that almost as soon as I took it.

The job required me to sit for long hours developing technical proposals, a task for which I did not have the attention span. I also really suck at writing technical proposals, possibly because I don't like sitting around developing them. My first set of proposals was lambasted, not because of the technical stuff, but because of the writing.

I also couldn't pick my projects. I was put on a team developing a point-of-sale solution for one of the national short-term loan companies (pawnshops). The more I learned about the business, the more I wanted out of there. Loaning money to the poor at 20 percent a month (not 20 percent a year, like credit card providers) made me ill.

Finally, I had really enjoyed my team in the briefing center, but my new team comprised mostly unhappy single people, unhappy divorced people and unhappy married people. Most of them had traveled too much in their careers and had poor personal relationships in their lives. Not fun. I missed my old team.

Then one day, about six months in, my young project manager attempted to humiliate me in front of the team for my poor writing skills. So I quit. I quit the project and I quit being a consultant.

It took me two months to find another position within the marketing division of IBM, but even as I took the job, I knew this was a holding place. Less than a year later, I left IBM after 22 years to go to work for a successful semi-conductor startup.

MISTAKE 2: TAKING MY DREAM JOB

Big mistake No. 2 was going full bore after what I believed to be my dream job. You know dream jobs: working in the embassy in Paris, owning a B&B, being a recruiter for the NFL. ... They look perfect, like career Valhalla, except most of us choose a dream job without ever investigating what it actually entails. We suffer from MSU (Making Stuff Up) Disorder, which we'll talk about in a later chapter. My dream job was more of the "To Sir, With Love," "Stand and Deliver," "Freedom Writers" variety. I went to teach high school math in an inner city school.

I had been developing curriculum and teaching engineers on and off for 20-plus years in about 35 different countries. Heck, if I could train engineers in the People's Republic of China, I was sure I could teach Algebra I and II to teenagers. And I could. But that's not all you have to know about the job you're going into.

First of all, no one told me that the average math teacher in Texas leaves the profession in fewer than five years. When I asked teachers about their experiences, they sugarcoated their answers. They didn't tell me that being an experienced 40-something can be a bad thing in a school system, where administrators prefer to deal with compliant, new grads. They didn't warn me that the hiring process was obscure and convoluted, and when I went through the alternative certification process at my local community college, my gut was telling me that I was not going to be prepared.

Most of all, I was not prepared for the trauma of working with a bunch of kids whose problems in life were far beyond what I could get my head around or do anything about. I thought that since I was an expert in multiple cultures, a veteran instructor and a tough guy, I could handle it. The culture of poverty introduced me to things beyond what I could handle.

I was good at what I did. I had a tremendous success rate and I touched many lives. That's the whole reason I went into the job in the first place. If that had been enough, I'd still be there. But the whole experience tore me up emotionally and physically. What made it worse was that the mentors who got me through the first year were all gone the next fall. I thought I could handle it without them. I was wrong. In hindsight, I should have quit at the end of my first year.

But I am a Baby Boomer. When we undertake to do a thing, we have to see it through or be a "quitter." I tried to follow the immortal words of Winston

Churchill: "Never, never, never give up." You stick it out until you have no choice but to leave. New information: When it comes to picking a job, you should give up before then.

I was often approached by former colleagues telling me that they planned to follow in my footsteps when they retired. Most dream jobs are mistakes waiting to happen.

MISTAKE 3: I CAN MAKE THIS WORK

The next of my mistakes was to take a job that was not optimal, telling myself I could make it work. I had gone into teaching to do something meaningful, and when I left I still wanted to do something meaningful. So I looked for a job with a nonprofit. Since I had spent a considerable amount of my previous 15 years in sales support, I thought I'd be great at a fundraising position. By the way—we have way too many nonprofits in Austin, most of which have either no salaried positions or very few.

I pursued jobs at organizations with missions aligned with my own values. But I got nowhere. I broadened my search to include nonprofits that were "close enough."

Soon, I was hired by the local Jewish community center to build a corporate giving program. It is a worthy organization, but I'd chosen it because it was a nonprofit with a job, not because it was doing something I was already excited about. Its mission, while good, isn't really aligned with what's important to me. And frankly, being a non-Jew as the face for a Jewish organization was ... interesting! Austin has very few Jewish-owned businesses, which made it even more difficult. Plus, I saw telltale signs of the impending great recession. All of the banks I approached were very friendly, but kindly showed me the door. I had a position that would eventually be eliminated. Finally, I was rapidly figuring out that I could not tolerate the dysfunctional behavior of nonprofits. I was used to getting things done, but that is not how things typically work in nonprofits.

After six months, I decided I would leave right after the big fall gala. I would take vacation and then turn in my resignation. I lasted a year, but I made the decision pretty early on that this was not for me. Despite what I told myself, I could not make it work.

FAILURE'S UPSIDE

Actually, I am happy I took all three jobs. I learned a tremendous amount about consulting, public education and nonprofits. I learned a lot about myself:

- My team is really important.

- I do not have unlimited energy to muscle through difficult situations.

- The mission is really important to me.

Very few of us just hop from one career into the perfect one without some experimentation.

My client Dave, for example, was a B2B sales guy. A lot of those types of jobs have disappeared because procurement experts do their own research on the internet, rather than having a salesperson explain why their option is better. So Dave started thinking about some other options. He had an associate's degree in aviation and decided to go back and get his bachelor's.

"If it has wings, wheels or keels," he said, "it's for me." Dave read a lot of articles about a guy who got a job on the British tube system and how he had prepared himself. Then he learned that the Houston Metro system was opening up its Red Line and needed train drivers. He got the job, and he loved it. But his wife still lived in Austin and he lived in Houston. So after a year, he started looking for something else.

Now he's preparing to become a drone pilot who teaches people how to fly them. Drones are used in so many things: construction, conservation, and agriculture just to name a few. The world is wide open for Dave, and he's having a lot of fun designing his pivot.

Failing, experimenting, and reinventing can be an adventure. But you need your infrastructure in place, which I lacked. I came up with a plan, based on my mistakes that can help anyone who is getting ready to make a Career Pivot.

RULES OF REINVENTION

HAVE A PLAN B: Be prepared to pull the plug on the reinvention project. Have a clear timeline and metrics to determine your success. For example, you might have five goals you're working on in terms of finances, skills learned or happiness. Give yourself short windows to achieve these and evaluate realistically. If you're not hitting them, it's time to rethink your plan.

Don't wait and develop your Plan B in the middle of taking a new job; have it in place from Day 1. Make sure the work you're doing is something that you could use to pivot into something else. The big fear is moving away from your skill set and falling behind without building anything you can use in your next job if this one doesn't work out. Keep your network fresh even as you're working in a new job or industry.

With the bad consulting job, I knew that I could find a position in the division I left within IBM. It took two months, and the consulting group did not push me to find anything quickly. That was a solid Plan B. With the teaching job, there was no Plan B.

I had left my tech job two years before, which meant that I was already out of date. With my nonprofit, I decided to leave several months before I actually did, and knew I wanted to take a few months to rest. In the fall, I was approached with three technology

61

opportunities. Quickly, I had multiple Plan Bs! I took a long vacation and was hired in December 2007 by a tech startup to develop a training and certification program.

Think through your Plan B carefully. I have had several clients who took "survival" jobs while they figured out what they wanted to do. But some of these survival jobs were with companies that had constantly changing schedules. One of my clients, Mike, did this. He took a job at a home supply discount store, thinking it would be fun to work there for a while. But because he never knew when he would be working from week to week, he could never schedule meetings with me, meetings with other people in his network or job interviews. The job turned out to be a trap.

If this sort of thing happens, you need a plan to escape.

LEARN FROM YOUR MISTAKES: The way you turn a mistake into something good is by learning from the experience. You always have to take stock of choices and actions from your past and what you can take away that will make tomorrow's choices and actions better. I learned a ton from my mistakes.

From the bad consulting job, I learned how important a team was to me, what kinds of work I don't like and that you have to do your homework before you take a job. I actually relearned all those lessons in teaching. But I also realized it stimulated my entrepreneurial juices to be in this old battleship called public education. I mentored my principal as we went through a high school redesign. It was clear to me that I would eventually work for myself to fix real-world problems. I also learned that I did not have the emotional stamina to work with teenagers who had problems most of us cannot even imagine.

At the nonprofit, I learned that I really need to understand how organizational rules apply to my job before I take it. I assumed that I could get groups within the organization to work with me, to do things differently, to think a little differently — boy, was I wrong! Working inside of a nonprofit was not for me.

FAILURE IS AN OPTION, BUT FAIL FAST: In the tech world, especially in Silicon Valley, there's the rallying cry "fail fast, fail often." If you have that mentality, it means you're someone who is going to take some risks and try for big things. This mentality is very hard for someone who grew up in the 1960s and 1970s to adopt. We were taught to be risk averse.

I had a discussion with a franchising consultant a couple of years ago. He told me about the people he met in 2002-2004 who had been laid off after the dot-com bubble had burst. Many of them had a lot of money in retirement accounts and were interested in starting franchises. He advised them to limit their investments in the franchise to 10 percent of their net worth. Even though many of them could afford to take the risk, they chose not to pursue it because they were terrified of failing. They were still too risk- averse to take the chance.

But the world has changed. If you were unemployed in the 1960s and did not find a job quickly, there was something wrong with you. Today, a massive percentage of the population has been touched by unemployment. Being unemployed is no longer a red flag on your record.

And a lot of people would rather start their own businesses than get another job where someone else has their hand on the lever of their success and failure. Before the early 2000s, the upfront investment to start a business was huge. Most people would need to get a significant loan. If you were to fail, the financial and personal consequences would be very big. That is why most of us became employees.

That's no longer the case. If you have a laptop, an internet connection and some hustle, you can start a business right now, no money down. In the last five years I have:

- Published two books without a publisher, selling a couple thousand copies.

- Created a website and blog that garner over 10,000 visitors a month without a major capital investment.

- Created a highly recognizable brand — Career Pivot.

All of this was done with a lot of sweat equity but a very small financial investment.

I belong to several technology meetups where new companies form almost overnight. Co-founders meet, hatch a plan for an app, sign up for Amazon Web Services, rent space at a co-working facility, and start developing the product. Total investment? Less than $10K. Ten years ago, the initial investment was probably closer to $1M or more.

And if you fail, it's not a catastrophe. But you should fail fast. In two of the three situations, I failed within six months. This greatly eased my recovery. When I forced myself to stick it out, the recovery was much more painful. You also get farther away from your skills and network.

I've talked to so many people who hung on to their reinvention until they could no longer make it. They have yet to recover. They stuck to it so long that their connections with their previous careers were lost. As the adage goes: "Don't cling to a mistake just because it took you so long to make it."

If you're not failing, you're not growing. But you have to be doing both. Have a plan, have a way to gauge whether it's working and jump ship when it isn't. Unlike with the Apollo mission, if you've planned it right, another ship will come along soon enough.

ACTION STEPS:

- ✓ Reflect on a time when you had a career failure.

- ✓ Write down how you recovered?

- ✓ Reflect on what you could have done differently?

- ✓ Look at whether you have ever taken risks, and, if not, do you have regrets about that?

For additional resources, check out:

Repurpose Your Career Resource Center
https://careerpivot.com/RYC-Resources/

DO YOU SUFFER FROM
MSU DISORDER?

My client Bill writes for a major financial company. When we were talking about his career change, he said wistfully: "My dream job is to write for 'The Economist'."

"Oh?" I responded. "How do you know? Do you know someone who works there?" He didn't.

Did he know whether it was considered a great place to work? What kind of hours did the company expected from employees? Was there the opportunity to advance? What about the culture? Did he know about turnover there, or the reputation of the management or executive team?

He didn't know any of that.

"So," I said, "how the heck do you know what it is like to work there?" "Well, I really don't," he responded. "They just write such great content. They cover the world, and they're so focused on important news and trends. I am just sure it would a wonderful place to work."

So he had read "The Economist" and fixated on working there as his dream job. In short, he was Making Stuff Up. ("Stuff" could also be replaced by a four-letter Germanic-Old English word I use sometimes.)

Making Stuff Up (MSU) is what most of us do when we don't have actual information. When there are holes or gaps in what we know, we just fill them in with things that seem to make sense based on our hopes or fears. Often, the ideas we stuff the gaps with have absolutely nothing to do with the reality of the situation.

In Judith Glaser's book "Conversational Intelligence: How Great Leaders Build Trust & Get Extraordinary Results," she discusses how the stories we make up have a significant impact on our careers. MSU can cause you to go after a job that would make you miserable, because you didn't really research the job itself. It can keep you from pursuing a great job, because you're afraid you're unqualified. It can cause you to give up on a job you're being considered for because you assume they weren't interested or didn't like you. And it can cause other people to lose confidence in you, because you present as irrefutable fact information that has no basis. In short, it means you make decisions based on the ghosts in your head, which is generally a bad idea.

We all make stuff up sometimes, when the information's not there. It's perfectly human. But when it comes to your career, don't do it.

THE PAIN WE CAUSE OURSELVES:
AWFULIZING

Bill made stuff up about a dream job. But many people make stuff up that "awfulizes" a situation. They don't know the facts, so they cook up a worst-case scenario, talk themselves into it, and proceed to freak out about the story they just made up.

Rhoda, a former CEO, applied for a job as chief operating officer of a national association. She was excited about the job and felt like the feeling was mutual. But then she didn't hear back from anyone. So she looked at the association's website for any clues about what might have happened. There she saw the smiling face of their senior vice president of operations. In seconds, Rhoda had a story going. They had changed their minds! They had hired someone else already! They just hadn't bothered to tell her about it. She contacted me in a panic, a whole scene playing out in her head like a movie.

"So," I asked her, "in absence of information, you decided to play detective?"

I recommended she call her contact at the company and ask about it. When she did, she learned that the senior vice president of operations was the guy she had applied to replace. He was leaving because he needed to take care of a family member. The company had decided to upgrade the position from senior vice president to COO — the role Rhoda had applied for that still wasn't filled. She never would have come up with that explanation on her own. Rhoda did get the job, by the way.

Another client, Marcos, really wanted to leave his job, but had to wait until his 55th birthday or he would lose $150,000 in pension benefits. He applied for a job, and the interview process took months. At several points during the process, and negotiating about the role, he would close with "I'm not sure I'm the right person for this job." And every time they came back with an answer that resolved his concerns. He wasn't toying with them; he just wanted to negotiate for what was important to him.

And they wanted him. I could tell. But each time, there was a lull between him saying, "I'm not the right person" and the response. At one point, he simply didn't hear from anyone for several weeks. He called me in a panic: "I've lost the job!"

"What do you mean?" I asked.

"I haven't heard from them for weeks. They finally gave up, I lost the job!"

"You don't know that," I said. "All you know is that you don't know what's happening. Why don't you call the recruiter?" He did. No answer. I still encouraged him not to awfulize what was happening but acknowledge that he just didn't know. As it turned out, the recruiter's mother had gotten very ill and he'd dropped everything to take care of her. By the way, Marcos got that job, too.

When my client, Susan, started a new job with a major drug company, she knocked the ball out of the park. They loved her. But when the division Susan worked for, which had around 200 people, announced a 30 percent headcount reduction, she went into panic mode. Fortunately, she only had to wait one day to learn from her boss that not only would she still have her job, but she was to lead a highly prized project. She ignored every sign that she was highly valued, even though there were a lot of signs. She just made stuff up in her head when she heard about the layoffs, which caused enormous stress.

THE DIRE PREDICTIONS
THAT DON'T COME TRUE

My client Tania works from home. Whenever she has meetings with her boss, she brings a list of activities she's been doing and he always criticizes them in a harsh, abusive way. It's gone on like this for years. She brings the list; he tears her down. The rest of their relationship is fine. One day I suggested she try not bringing the list. After all, according to her, he'd never asked for a list. She only brought it because she'd done so with other bosses. She thought my suggestion was crazy. If she didn't bring the list, she assured me, he'd really come after her.

"How do you know?" I asked her. She didn't. She was Making Stuff Up.

71

Finally she screwed up her courage and went to the meeting without the list. She was kind of a basket case during the days before the meeting. But when she got there, without the list, he said nothing. He just took notes on her activities and didn't give her grief about it.

Tania's situation is another form of MSU I hear all the time: if/then

.

- If I raise the price, they'll stop hiring me.

- If I ask to change my hours, they'll fire me.

- If I refuse to take on extra hours, they'll give all the good projects to someone else.

But then I ask: "How do you know? On what information, what data, are you basing this assumption?" Usually it's just the ghosts in our heads. We don't know at all.

Often our MSU thoughts seem so real, or we've rehearsed them so often, that we don't even remember that we never stopped to ask "Where did I get this idea?"

We just get really anxious about something and it makes us feel like we have control if we can "decide" the outcome, even if it's totally made up. In fact, the only thing you can control is your response to the fact that you DON'T KNOW. So either find a way to get information or find a way to learn to live with uncertainty. There's a lot of that in life.

Learning to live with it is a good idea.

LET HISTORY GUIDE YOU

One thing that's really important with MSU is to make a mental bookmark of all the times you've been panicked about something and it turned out you were wrong. Think back to all the times you've awfulized something. Someone didn't call within a given window (that you made up) and you assumed something terrible had happened or was about to happen. You may have freaked out, chewed your nails, yelled at your family, drank a bunch of whiskey, applied for another job you really didn't want or eaten an entire cheesecake. Whatever. You could feel the tension rise inside you.

And the truth turned out to be nothing like the story you made up.

It's important to go back and remember those moments and how silly you felt afterward. The best thing to do in those situations is realize that you don't know what's happening, make an effort to get answers and breathe through the moment. Admitting you don't know is a lot less crazy-making than the intense fantasies you're likely to come up with. Try to stay in the moment and accept that the truth is you don't know. And that's OK.

STOP, DROP AND ROLL

Of course, it's hard to remember to breathe and stay in the moment when something big is on the line. That's why I suggest you remember "stop, drop and roll." Do you remember when, as a kid, you were told to stop, drop and roll should your clothes ever catch on fire? The idea was that your natural reaction to having fire on your body would be to panic and run, which would only make things worse. This easy-to-remember saying told you exactly what to do. So, before panic could set in, you'd stop, drop and roll.

Many of us have triggers that set off panic. My client Mary has a boss who tends to be rude whenever she calls. One day, Mary was attending a conference, quite happily listening to a session when she felt her cell phone vibrate. She looked down at the caller ID: It was her boss. This was usually a trigger for anxiety. She was going to get yelled at. Normally she would bolt out of the session and take the call, even though it was likely to be unpleasant.

This time, she remembered stop, drop and roll. She did not know why her boss was calling. She did not know whether she'd done anything that would get her yelled at. All she knew was that she was in a session and her boss was calling. So this time she did not immediately answer; she let the call go to voicemail. She texted her boss back saying she was sitting in a session and could not take her call. She then asked whether there was anything she could help her with.

Her boss replied that she too was coming to the conference and just wanted Mary to know. That was it. That was all.

Mary executed stop, drop and roll flawlessly. She controlled the narrative rather than letting her boss dictate her emotional state.

MANAGING COMMUNICATION

When my client Nancy took the job she has now, the boss admitted to Nancy that she was difficult to work for. So Nancy avoids the boss and only talks to her when something goes wrong. In between times, she makes up stuff in her head like:

I am not doing a good job. My boss does not like me.

They are setting me up to let me go.

Is any of this stuff true? I do not know ... and neither does Nancy.

I help people find new careers, but I also can help them find more satisfaction from the jobs they already have. Nancy really likes her job, aside from the constant panic that she's not doing well. So Nancy and I decided she should schedule a weekly meeting with her boss to discuss the following week's schedule. Nancy needed to talk to her boss on her own terms. She needed to manage the communication to find out what her boss really thinks. What she learned was that her boss is moody and that most of the time her behavior toward Nancy has nothing to do with Nancy. Opening up that conversation and understanding where her boss was coming from solved a lot of Nancy's MSU.

Everybody has MSU. Even scientists and engineers who aren't supposed to ever make stuff up. It's a normal thing our brain does. The problem isn't that we make up a story. The problem is that we believe it and react to it. Instead, we need to recognize that MSU is just our brain filling in the holes and that it might not be true at all. So stop, drop and roll. Don't get upset about the story in your head. Take a deep breath and get facts, or just admit you don't know.

One of the big issues for people in a career transition is learning to deal with the uncertainty. But you can deal with uncertainty while looking for what you really want or while gritting your teeth and putting up with a job you really don't. I think the first one's better.

ACTION STEPS:

- ✓ Describe a time or times when you "made stuff up."

- ✓ Develop a "stop, drop and roll" to apply in each situation where you tend to make stuff up.

For additional resources, check out:

Repurpose Your Career Resource Center
https://careerpivot.com/RYC-Resources/

THE HARDEST PART:
ASKING FOR HELP

Believe it or not, often the hardest part of shifting careers or making changes within your career is asking for help.

I admit it – I am a guy. I do not like asking for help. I do not like asking for directions. There, I said it. Sometimes, we're thrust into situations where our choices are to quit or ask for help. You know you have been there!

You can't do this alone. No matter how many books, articles or blogs you read, you will have to talk to real people in the world you're seeking to enter. The people in your industry or the company you are targeting are the ones who can tell you about the top players in the industry, the unspoken rules and the most-tested paths to success. They're the ones who can introduce you to the right people, put in a good word for you or steer you away from the kinds of people who can sabotage your efforts.

A LITTLE HUMBLE PIE WITH YOUR COFFEE?

In these transactions, you're the receiver, the seeker, the newbie — not the expert. The lunch you bought your source doesn't adequately compensate him or her for the knowledge you're getting. You're not in the power position. That's hard for people who have achieved success in their careers and a certain number of gray hairs on their heads.

For most of us guys, it can actually be a pretty miserable experience. I was a very experienced professional and used to succeeding. I had never really failed miserably at anything until I got the teaching gig. When I did fail miserably there, I wanted to just quit.

Because I didn't believe I should quit, I sucked it up and asked for help. It was hard. But it was eye opening and I ended up being an almost religious supporter of the notion that people really only get where they're going with the help of other people.

Here's the shocker: Most people are happy to help you. For one thing, people generally like to be helpful.

For another, you are offering them the power position, and that feels good to everyone. Think of giving the other person that role as a gift. As long as you pay the tab for the coffee or the meal and send them a thank-you note afterward, both of you will benefit from your session.

When I went off to teach high school math, I had a great Algebra I mentor. I was totally lost teaching Algebra II. After a few weeks, I asked Ginny, a 27-year-old Algebra II teacher, if I could use her lesson plans. My plan was to stay two days behind her in the curriculum and follow her lead exactly. That way I could go down and watch her teach any lesson that I did not understand. I played little puppy dog the rest of the year. Everything she did, I did. I was old enough to be her father, but I followed her lead.

I sucked it up and asked for help.

And it gets easier. Not everyone will have insights that move you forward, but just practicing asking for help is an enormously powerful thing.

There are several areas where job seekers may need help:

RESEARCHING POTENTIAL CAREERS

- Asking someone on the inside what it's really like to work in a specific field.

- Asking someone on the inside what it's like to work for a specific company, and what it takes to get in and succeed.

- Asking for advice about what's needed in a specific career.

- Asking for a recommendation or introduction to someone who can give you more advice.

SEEKING SUPPORT

- Asking for a recommendation on your resume or LinkedIn.

- Asking for someone to put in a good word for you.

SOCIAL MEDIA HELP

Nowadays, there are so many social networks that people are getting picky about which ones they want to mess with. You need to figure out where the people you need to talk to are.

LinkedIn is a given. When hiring, many companies now look at a LinkedIn profile in lieu of a resume. But there are also a lot of Facebook groups around finding jobs and networking, so it's useful to be active there, too.

The bottom line is you don't have to know all the tools, apps and social media sites, but you do have to have enough familiarity with them to be ready to learn a new one fast when someone asks you to use it to set up an appointment, apply for a job or complete some other task. Try Googling "top job-seeking applications and software" to see what's hot right now.

ALL IS NOT LOST

Probably, the skills and experience you've amassed over your career will find a place in your new career and help you be even better at your new job than you would have been without them.

But right now, clinging to the security of competency you've demonstrated at your old job will just get in the way of finding a new career you can enjoy for the next several decades.

Depending on the magnitude of the pivot you intend to make, you will have to suck it up and be humble. You are no longer the expert. I have a friend who is making a major change into green energy. He is working as an apprentice electrician. He is learning to be humble.

When he's done, he'll have new knowledge that—coupled with everything he's learned about working hard, meeting customers' expectations and marketing himself—will take him into a future he wants.

He will have made the pivot. After all, that's the goal.

ACTION STEPS:

✓ Find people who can help you reach those goals and connect with them via LinkedIn, email or phone call.

✓ Take these people out for coffee, lunch or a walk. Remember to be humble. This time, you're not the expert!

For additional resources, check out:

Repurpose Your Career Resource Center
https://careerpivot.com/RYC-Resources/

BUILDING YOUR TRIBE

Networking is the way everything works. That old saying is true: "It's not what you know; it's who you know." But exchanging business cards and a LinkedIn connection is just scratching the networking surface. Many of these superficial connections will have no impact on your search.

The people who will make a difference are your tribe. It's fine to have 500-plus LinkedIn connections. But it's crucial to have a group of people with whom you have actual relationships, who are interested in helping you reach your goals and who depend on you to help them reach theirs. I have a rather large network, but my tribe consists of about 150 people.

Your tribe is the group of people who will get you through your Career Pivot. Believe me, while you're coping with all this change, facing uncertain prospects and being humble while asking for help, you need people rooting for you. Your tribe is also the group you can call on for an introduction or some advice over coffee. And they can call on you, too—whether for themselves or for a friend who wants some intelligence about your areas of expertise. It's like a community barn-raising: You help your neighbor build his barn, knowing—without asking—he'll show up with lunch and a hammer to help you raise yours.

A TRIBE WILL GET YOU THROUGH THIS

When I was a teacher, I began sending regular emails to friends and other teachers about my experiences. I talked about the kids who seemed overwhelmed and the strategies I devised to help them. I talked about their low self-esteem and the issues they were struggling to overcome, and how hard it was to communicate something as abstract as algebra in the midst of their concrete problems. I learned that many people I sent those emails to forwarded them to friends and family members in the school district. I unwittingly built a tribe of people who were rooting for me, and for my kids, throughout those hard years. I couldn't have made it without them.

Don't try something as challenging as a Career Pivot without a tribe.

CULTIVATE YOUR TRIBE

The thing about a tribe is, you have to cultivate it, like a garden. You need to weed it from time to time of people you have no real connection with. You have to water it when there's no rain. You may need to apply fertilizer. Most importantly, you should not neglect it. You need to give it TLC. It needs to be part of the way you think and live, or it will wither.

Do you have friends you have not seen in months? Take a day each week to reach out with an email and check-in. At least once a week, I glance through LinkedIn or Outlook contacts and find someone I have not heard from in a while. Then I send a check-in email.

It could be as simple as:

Bob,

I have not heard from you in a while. How are you doing? How is your family? Things are going well with my business. Son is getting married in October ...

Let me know how you're doing. Do you want to meet for a cup of coffee sometime soon?

Marc

The response is often:

Marc,

Thanks for checking in with me. Life is good ... Too busy to meet for coffee but check back in ... Bob

I now know how he is doing and he knows that I care about him. Networking is all about building relationships. Are you cultivating your network?

Are you doing something new and original that you would like to share?

There is no substitute for face-to-face meetings to establish and maintain relationships. I like social media, but that good old face-to-face meeting where you get to shake hands and read body language is critical to long-term relationships.

When do you have the time to do this?

MAKE IT A HABIT

I like to have coffee meetings at 7 or 7:30 a.m. When our son was small, I learned it was easy for me to keep that hour clear for networking. My wife, boss, teammates and son could schedule things for me to do at any other time. But first thing in the morning was sacred. Sometimes a "coffee meeting" doesn't involve meeting for coffee. Here in Austin, people often meet while walking around Lady Bird Lake in the center of town. It might even be for a game of tennis or similar sport. But no matter what I'm doing, it's about the connection.

What time works for you? Lunch? After work for a beer or other libation? Or maybe Saturdays?

Pick a time — once a week, once every two weeks or once a month — to meet face to face with someone in your network. Make it a pattern.

LET KARMA DO ITS THING

When you network, it is all about the other person, and you should expect nothing in return. When I am meeting with someone and if I determine I can be of some help, I just do it. Cultivating good karma will always pay off somewhere. Don't ask for it. Your payback will happen in a way that's better than what you might have asked for.

Recently, I met with my image consultant, Jean LeFebvre, to order a new shirt. Jean told me she was looking for client companies that cared about how their employees dressed and would be willing to hire someone to make them look spiffy. In Austin, casual is king, so she didn't have many prospects. The one industry we could agree met her criteria was the legal field. Austin is the state capital; we have lots of lawyers.

I offered to introduce Jean to Susan Baughman, who has a business called Lawyers Don't Know Marketing. Susan creates custom marketing programs for law firms.

I sent Susan an email with the subject line "Virtual Introduction" and copied Jean. I explained Jean's situation and asked Susan if she could help. As it turns out, Susan was looking for an image consultant for her clients and was willing to educate Jean on the art of dealing with law firms in Austin.

Making this kind of connection isn't just a fluke. Part of cultivating your tribe is looking for opportunities to do things like this for other people and not expecting anything in return. It's goodwill, good karma. Somewhere down the road, it will come back to you.

In the situation I mentioned about connecting my two friends, one of them may one day be dealing with an attorney who wants to make a career shift, and, instead of just listening sympathetically to the attorney's frustration, she'll introduce them to me. Who knows? The point is, cultivating good karma as a habit will always pay off somewhere.

DON'T FORGET TO SAY THANK YOU

If someone makes a connection for you, don't forget to send a quick note or email to tell them what happened and thank them.

Dear Barb,

Thank you so much for introducing me to Stephen. We have connected over coffee and found several places where our business objectives might lead to really fruitful partnerships.

I don't know if we would have ever discovered each other without your help. Thanks for taking the time to do that!

Leslie

People don't need a reward for helping you. But you should give them the gift of letting them know that they did, in fact, help.

Building your tribe, cultivating it and giving it TLC might be the most valuable and enriching part of making a Career Pivot.

ACTION STEPS:

- ✓ Connect regularly with members of your tribe, friends and associates. They provide emotional support and may have leads for you.

- ✓ Thank them promptly with a note for any help they give you and let them know the outcome of their help.

- ✓ Seek ways to help others in their career or business goals without asking anything in return. Karma works.

For additional resources, check out:

Repurpose Your Career Resource Center
https://careerpivot.com/RYC-Resources/

HOW TO NETWORK STRATEGICALLY

What the heck is strategic networking? It is networking with a defined goal and a strategy to get to that goal. For example:

- You are unemployed and your goal is a job in a specific company that pays well and treats employees well. Your strategy might be to cozy up to the recruiter or hiring manager for a specific company.

- Your goal is to decide on a new career path. Your strategy is to meet and learn from professionals in the field that you wish to switch into.

- Your goal is to move up or laterally in your current company. Your strategy is to meet and build relationships outside of your current management chain.

Strategic networking is building relationships with people who can help you obtain that next professional position. They might be in a specific industry or even a specific company within that industry. The strategic part is finding contacts in those industries or companies who can connect you with new contacts. These might be employees, executives or recruiters.

NETWORKING WITH A RECRUITER

Having connections with multiple recruiters is useful in your job search but also in managing your career. Recruiters go from company to company, moving with hiring trends. This is particularly true of contract recruiters, and they carry their connections with them. Don't be intimidated to approach recruiters. They have this job because they like helping people find jobs that work.

Recruiters are usually connected on LinkedIn to the vast majority of the personnel within the organizations they support. They also accept links to potential candidates readily. One last tip about recruiters: They'll usually use a company email address on LinkedIn. From their address, you can figure out how the company formats it email addresses (for example, jane.doe@company.com or jdoe@company.com). This helps you guess the emails of other employees you may want to contact.

Locate a recruiter at the target company and connect with him or her. If you are a viable candidate, the recruiter will want to connect. If not, try a different recruiter at the same company. If the recruiter does connect, call her. Here's what to say:

- If you are looking at a specific job, ask which recruiter is handling the position.

- If you are looking at a specific area within the company, ask which recruiter is handling that specific area.

- Ask about the culture and opportunities within the company.

If the recruiter does not answer, leave a message with your questions and follow up with an email. Be persistent and repeat this procedure in a few days if you don't get a response.

STRATEGIC NETWORKING WITH AN INDIVIDUAL

What if you want to meet an individual in a company who might be able to help you reach your goals? Let's say his name is Jeffrey. Do you contact Jeffrey and ask him for an "informational interview"? That's how some people do it. But I don't like the term "informational interview." It says "I want a JOB," which scares people off.

ASK FOR A – I – R

A–Advice. When you ask for advice, it is a compliment. Rarely will anyone turn you down when you ask advice. In the email, ask for 30 minutes of Jeffrey's time to ask for some advice. It could be about how to pursue a position at the company or to learn more about the company. The magic word is *advice*!

I – Insights. Once you meet Jeffrey, ask for his insights into how the company functions, the culture and the management structure.

R – Recommendations. This is what many people forget. Ask questions like these: "What should I do next? Is there anyone else you would recommend I talk with? Can you introduce me to anyone else within the organization?"

You will ask Jeffrey questions and only talk about yourself when asked. You have not asked for help to get a job, only for help in understanding the organization and for further networking opportunities. You are networking to build relationships and not to find a job. The opportunity to interview for a position will come later, after you have established relationships. Jeffrey will likely provide an introduction to at least one person if you made it clear you were interested in him and his perspective.

Again, this is not about you!

ABOUT CONNECTORS

Some people pride themselves on being connectors. I am one such person. We're not recruiters or HR people; we just enjoy helping people along their career paths and we're good at making relationships with a lot of different people.

We attend a lot of functions, eagerly meet new associates and remember to pull out your name when we hear someone speaking about needing someone with your skills, attributes or background.

We are worth cultivating because our hobby is so helpful to other people. If you know someone you think is a connector, take the time and trouble to take that person to coffee and ask for AIR. Who knows what it will lead to?

NEXT STEP, SEND THANK-YOU NOTES

Never forget to send thank-you emails as you move forward in your strategic networking.

Send a thank-you note to Ann who introduced you to Jeffrey. Ann will want to know the outcome of your meeting with Jeffrey.

Send a thank you note to Jeffrey.

And then let's say Jeffrey introduces you to Paul. After you meet with Paul, do the following:

Send a note to Jeffrey to let him know the outcome of your meeting with Paul. Send a note to Ann to let her know that you met with Paul.

Send a thank-you note to Paul.

If Paul introduces you to Mary, after meeting with Mary you send a note to Ann, Jeffrey, Paul and Mary. After each meeting, you send a note to everyone who helped you get there.

Yes, EVERYONE.

It really bugs me when I make an introduction for someone and I find out six months later that it led them down a chain of events that had a positive outcome and no one told me. Please come back and tell me.

Strategic networking is building RELATIONSHIPS with people who can help you obtain that next professional position. If you go back and thank the person who helped you, you deepen the relationship.

Frequently, the only benefit the person who helped you derives from the interaction is the knowledge he helped someone. But that is a great feeling. It releases dopamine, a brain chemical connected with reward. It gives him a boost in his day. And it keeps him from wondering if he made a terrible mistake. Let him know what happened.

Moreover, as you progress forward, you might make a connection that is helpful to the people who helped you get there.

Don't be surprised if you, the person asking for help, very quickly becomes the one offering it.

ACTION STEPS:

- ✓ Network with recruiters and individuals — especially people who like to be connectors —who can help you toward your goals through LinkedIn and networking events.

- ✓ Don't ask for an informational interview or even for help finding a job. Instead, buy them lunch or coffee and ask only for AIR (Advice, Insights and Recommendations).

- ✓ Thank everyone who helps and let them know the outcome of their help.

For additional resources, check out:

Repurpose Your Career Resource Center
https://careerpivot.com/RYC-Resources/

HOW JOB HUNTING IS LIKE DATING

Managing your career is a lot like dating and marriage. This is coming from a guy who has been married for over 30 years. Everyone assures me that I'm not missing anything— I really do not want to date again.

Frequently, we date the same way we look for a job. We put our best foot forward and pray they won't reject us. If that's all you're doing, if you aren't also deciding whether you really want to be stuck with them, you can wind up with some lousy partners — and jobs.

Every date does not turn into marriage. It's only after lots of dates, when you are sure that the two of you are compatible, that a good marriage can happen. The same thing happens when you go in for an interview.

Another similarity is that waxing bitter about your previous relationships will not produce good results. If you complain about your current managers, just like if you gripe about your exes, you're likely to get scratched off the list.

Thirty years ago I was working for IBM as a computer programmer. The project I worked on was fraught with problems. So I submitted an application for a position with a major computer software company. I got the interview, but after about 20 minutes I knew they would not hire me. I was extremely negative and I never heard from them again.

If you are angry or miserable, you absolutely need to get past that. Focus on what you want and where you want to go. Think of the light at the end of the tunnel.

Can you picture where you want to go? What does it look like? Let's start by describing the boss you'd love to have.

I have many clients who want and very much need someone who is collegial, almost a peer. I have other clients who very much want someone who is in control. But I most commonly see the desire to have a boss who is politically astute and gives my client complete control to do what needs to get done.

My favorite boss was Theresa, who managed the IBM AIX Briefing Center in Austin. She was phenomenally good at hiring superstars and then leaving them alone to do their jobs. If anything went wrong or there was political conflict, she was right there to back us up. She was not competent, though, to make technical decisions, so she left those to her team. Best manager I have ever had.

I have often talked to young engineers who assumed their bosses were better engineers than they were and teachers who assumed the principals must have been fantastic in the classroom. Neither of those is true. The skill set needed for your job may not mirror the skills a manager needs.

Who has been your best boss? What made that boss so good?

You need to craft the equivalent of an elevator pitch to say, "This is what I am looking for." You need to clearly and succinctly express what you want.

What size organization suits you best? What kind of environment is the best soil for you to work in? What kind of culture and organizational structure do you want? Create an elevator speech that defines all of that:

I am looking for a smaller organization in the xxx industry, where I get to lead a cohesive team developing yyy. I want a manager who will support me but allow me to run the show as I see fit. I want to work in an organization that values teamwork with minimal politics ...

How long will this pitch take to develop and perfect? Probably longer than you think.

You will need to practice it on friends, significant others and anyone else who will provide constructive criticism.

Once you have crafted your "Here is what I want" pitch, get out and talk to people. When you can state clearly and succinctly what you want, friends and colleagues will come to your aid. This is a real key to future happiness: Know what you want, and know how to ask for it.

DATING IS TRYING PEOPLE OUT

I had a client who took a retirement package from a tech company and decided he wanted to try something completely new. He wanted to be a butcher. I don't remember why. I think it had something to do with desiring hands-on work, becoming an artisan, liking meat, remembering the role of butchers in his neighborhood. At any rate, he had the smarts to "date" butchery as a career choice.

He took a couple of animal husbandry classes and then he got a seasonal job in the meat department at a boutique grocery. From that experience, he learned that he did not like being on his feet all day on concrete floors.

He "dated" the job he was interested in instead of moving in right away.

Remember, any job you take is a commitment, even if you don't stay in it very long. It's a lot of work to get hired, get in the system, let go of other searches and then recover if it doesn't work out. Take your time at the front rather than having to clean up a lot of mess on the other end.

ACTION STEPS:

- ✓ Start thinking about job seeking in terms of dating. You won't just take whoever will have you; you're looking for a good fit, too.

- ✓ Craft a pitch succinctly stating exactly what you want: "I want an executive position with a lot of autonomy in a small, but thriving, HR firm."

- ✓ Share your pitch with everyone you meet.

For additional resources, check out:

Repurpose Your Career Resource Center
https://careerpivot.com/RYC-Resources/

YOUR PERSONAL BRAND

For Baby Boomers, it's weird to think about having a personal brand. We grew up with brands: peanut butter brands, coffee brands, car brands. By creating a personal brand it's like we're designating ourselves as products, with a logo sticker and an expiration date. And in a sense, we are.

Back in the day, we didn't need personal brands. We just had reputations. Your co-workers, social circles and family knew your reputation. But unless you were some kind of public figure — or someone who waxed eloquent on the bathroom wall — your reputation wasn't widely known.

You were known for your accomplishments as well as the way you treated other people. It was crucial that others noticed your good work. If you sat in the corner, did a good job and kept your nose clean, you still might remain invisible to the organization. Only if you worked on a critical piece of the project would anyone outside of your immediate team know what you did. Your reputation was known mostly within your group, team or project. If you moved from project to project, your reputation often followed you.

Let's fast forward to the 21st century. With the rise of the internet and social media came the concept of personal brand. Now, if you have a Facebook or Twitter account, you have a reputation not only with friends and family, but things you post might also be reposted before strangers. If you take strong political stands, then you're known as a community-minded person or a blowhard, depending on the perspective of the person who sees your posts. If you post your daily activities and photos of all your meals, that may communicate you have too much time on your hands, are lonely or need validation. If you post off-color jokes, that tells people something about you, too.

These days, everyone is so busy, there is so much information available, that the only way to get seen by the people you want to recognize you is to create a visible presence. If you don't, the next guy will, and you'll be overlooked.

Interestingly, not having social media accounts also says something about you. These days, if people Google you and you have no online presence, it can communicate that you are:

1) Too much of an old fuddy-duddy to participate in contemporary society or

2) Hiding something.

Being invisible online means you're not part of the conversation. And if you're trying to pivot your career, not having a LinkedIn account is like sending out your resume in invisible ink. LinkedIn is where people connect over work. If you're not there, with a strong personal brand, the people who could get you where you want to be may never find you.

I hate the new world order!

Many of you may be saying, "I do not have time for this! All this posting and reputation building and interacting with people about things I barely care about!"

I get where you're coming from, but unfortunately, you probably have to make time. Learning to navigate the social media world is like learning to use the internet. You can't operate effectively without it. But you only have to use the parts of it that actually serve your purpose. You don't have to post pictures of your lunch, for instance.

Many of you may also be really uncomfortable with promoting yourself. Growing up, many of us were taught that self-promotion is improper. We were assured that we just needed to work hard to be recognized and that any effort to attract attention to ourselves was immodest. Women were especially taught that lesson, and were shocked by books like "Games Mother Never Taught You: Corporate Gamesmanship for Women" that came out in 1977 saying women needed to go after their share of recognition to get ahead in the corporate world. Dan Schawbel's "Promote Yourself" is a modern counter to that modesty training.

The good news is that if you make an effort, you can be seen and recognized by people you never had the opportunity to reach before. The question is, what message do you want to reach them with? What's your personal brand?

YOUR BRAND STORY

Where does your brand story come from? From you. When I meet a client, he tells me his story. Where he grew up, how he grew up, where he worked, jobs he's had, which ones he liked and which he hated and why. I can always hear threads that run through his story. As a recovering engineer — one of my brand statements — I recognize patterns.

One client I have is a product manager. All his life, he's loved taking other people's visions and making them happen. Even before becoming a product manager, he ran an annual parade and created floats that other people designed. He was, he realized, the vision enabler. He brings ideas into focus and makes them a reality.

But even though he knew some of this, when I repeated it back to him after he told me his story, he could see himself from a new perspective. He understood himself in a way he hadn't before. And it helped him define the extra value he brings to organizations he works for—his brand.

Your story isn't your resume. It is who you are, not what you have done. It should convey what you stand for, your morals and values, your personality and passions.

I have taken several online programs that were supposed to help me develop a brand story. What I discovered was that I was really lousy at creating and writing my own brand story. I've had a couple clients work this online process, too, but they did not do any better. In fact, most didn't finish. Why is this?

Part of it is that many of us are uncomfortable with what feels like excessive navel- gazing. But the other piece is, we do not see ourselves the way other people see us! Most of us have huge blind spots when it comes to our reputations. We need other people to reflect what they see before we can really understand our brands.

The worst person to write your brand story is you!

Do marketing professionals sit quietly in a room by themselves and dream up brand ideas? No! They collaborate. They brainstorm and bounce ideas off one another. When working on your brand and story, get outside help and feedback. I work with clients in a systematic way to develop their brand stories:

FIND YOUR THEMES

We all have themes running through our lives. But many of us have difficulty seeing those themes. We are just too close! Work with a good friend, relative or even a career professional who can help you identify your themes. Talk about your story and don't edit! See what threads the other person sees running through your life.

Frequently, your story may have one pivotal moment. For me, it was my bicycle accident. For one of my clients, it was taking ballet as a teenager.

Sometimes, really honest people may see things you're not real thrilled about — like that you've always had personality conflicts with the boss or that you've quit jobs too often or stayed in them long after you knew you hated them. Face those things too. Don't fall prey to your blind spots. This may be a bit painful, but our greatest lessons and later victories are often tied to experiences that came out of dark times.

On the other hand, just because it's an outside perspective doesn't mean it's accurate. Only seek this help from someone you trust and make sure what the other person is saying resonates with you.

LABEL YOURSELF

Work with the same people who helped you develop a theme to create a label that defines you. Have fun with this! Ask friends questions like "What words describe me?" and "If I were an animal, which animal would I be?"

Think about brand slogans like Nike's "Just Do It," "You're in Good Hands With Allstate" or Capital One's "What's In Your Wallet?" Your label is your personal tagline. It has to be very tight. Think of it as the line at the top of your LinkedIn profile: That's only 200 characters.

Find the statement that accurately describes you and then look for the perfect words. I had great fun with a client looking through the thesaurus to come up with the label "I am the confluence of business and art."

Another client loves making things happen and making dreams come true for people. I told her she should be "the fairy godmother." But for her, that conjured up pictures of Disney's "Cinderella." To her, "fairy godmother" said "purple and fat." So we had to find a different brand label. We finally came up with "the playmaker." She likes to make the plays. She could have been "the quarterback."

Even when you get an accurate label, it may feel a little uncomfortable at first — like a new haircut. The question is, does it really tell people, in a few words, what your big value-add is?

Label yourself with a phrase that is memorable. For instance, I used to refer to myself as an articulate techno-weenie, but I now refer to myself as a recovering engineer.

A client of mine has created this label: "I'm a cause-driven, people-oriented geek." Your story and label should enforce what you want people to remember about you. Come up with a memorable phrase that authentically says who you are. You don't want marketing that sounds great but doesn't really tell who you are. Find a group of your friends who can brainstorm on the topic and share what they think is a true expression of who you are and what you bring to the table. Come up with 20-30 phrases, and then test them out vocally. You have to be comfortable using the phrase.

For my client who loves to create order out of chaos we came up with "structured anarchist."

Ultimately, you're creating your brand to share with the world so you can attain the career you want. But this exercise can also be really great at just clarifying and validating what you've been learning and producing thus far in your career and life — what your value is to the places where you contribute. And that, alone, is a great reason to take the plunge and find your brand.

ACTION STEPS:

- ✓ Find someone who can help you with your brand story. This could be a friend, relative or paid professional.

- ✓ Brainstorm with this person on what should be the common theme for your brand story.

- ✓ Allow someone else to write or co-write your brand story.

For additional resources, check out:

Repurpose Your Career Resource Center
https://careerpivot.com/RYC-Resources/

VETTING THE COMPANY

I have a client who told me that she had interviewed with one of the very sexy startups in town about six months earlier. She got to the finals and lost. So I asked why she wanted to work at that startup. It had a horrid reputation for hiring people and quickly chewing them up. My client acknowledged that the candidate who was hired was fired six weeks later. When they approached my client about the position after the firing, my client said, "No thanks!"

Before approaching a company about a job, do your due diligence:

- Research the company on sites like Glassdoor.com.

- Check LinkedIn for recommendations. Go to the hiring manager's profile and check his or her recommendations section:

- Have they given recommendations to their employees?

- Have their employees recommended their manager?

- Check other profiles within the organization to determine if there is a culture of giving recommendations on LinkedIn. If that is not in the company's culture, it's a bad sign. You find this culture more commonly, by the way, in newer and smaller organizations than in big multinational companies.

- Connect with recruiters or HR professionals at the target company on LinkedIn. This will give you visibility to the organization needed.

- Target former employees who have personal relationships with people you know. Ask around among your connections to see if anyone has a personal relationship with your target employee and would be comfortable giving an introduction.

Former employees are incredibly valuable and often will give you an honest evaluation of what it is to work at a company.

One of my clients, Steven, was interviewing for a high-level HR position with a technology company that had just gone public. Steven reached out to three former employees and asked them why they left. All three responded with the same answer — the toxic work environment. Steven had the interview and the tech company made an offer. Steven turned them down. We later found out the company had many internal issues and there was high turnover.

Find out what current and former employees think of the hiring manager. Current employees who work for the hiring manager might be evasive or not truthful. Be aware of their body language. Former employees will likely be more forthcoming with the truth.

PREPARE FOR THE INTERVIEW

The interview is like the first date. And on the first date, it's not all about whether the other person likes you. What do you like or not like about the company? Are you ready with your elevator speech about what you need?

This interview isn't just about whether you get the job. It is about whether you want the job. A small business owner told me that she always starts interviews with "Do you have any questions about the position?" If the candidate says no, then the interview is pretty much over. She wants to hire people who are looking for her company, not just "a job."

Come into any interview with at least 10 questions. Print them out and keep them in front of you. Take notes and write the interviewer's answers on the paper. This gives you time to think about where to take the conversation next!

Controlled pauses like these give you a chance to think about the flow of the conversation. Another example of a controlled pause is to restate the question you were just asked. "Let me make sure I understand your question. You asked .... "

Among your questions should be:

- What is the management style of the hiring manager?

- What is the team environment like?

- What is the reward structure?

- How structured is the work environment?

- How much freedom is allowed to do the job the way you want to do it?

You will likely interview with peers of the hiring manager, upper-level managers and peers of the position you are pursuing. Use the first two questions with each. Beware that your future peers may be deceptive. Also, look for very different answers coming from different levels of management. My last manager was amazing at managing up and lousy at managing down. His management team had a very different opinion of him than the people he managed. Look for discrepancies. When you interview with the hiring manager, ask the following questions:

- Describe your management style.

- Give me three words that describe you at work.

- What do you like best about being a manager?

Most hiring managers are not very good at interviewing. Most have never been trained on interviewing skills. When you take this approach, they often like it. If the hiring manager balks at any of these questions, you might want to dig deeper.

Sometimes you will have to dig and read body language to get an accurate gauge on the situation. Given the information you have received from current and former employees, you should be able to play detective.

Pay attention to your gut instincts. If it does not feel right, it is probably not a good fit. Have you ever not followed your instincts and regretted it? It all comes down to you taking responsibility for the process.

ACTION STEPS:

✓ Check out the company before the interview. Look on sites like Glassdoor.com and talk to people who work for the company and former employees to learn about the culture.

✓ Look at the company's employee's LinkedIn pages to see if they give and receive recommendations. This could be a sign of the company's level of supportiveness.

✓ Prepare a list of at least 10 questions you want answered before you decide to take the job.

For additional resources, check out:

Repurpose Your Career Resource Center
https://careerpivot.com/RYC-Resources/

THE DREADED QUESTION

It is all but guaranteed that somewhere in the interview process you will be asked the following question:

"Why do you want to leave your current position?"

Prepare an answer, of course, but also prepare for the interviewer to keep harping on the question in one form or another to see if you will start spilling angry beans. Have a strategy against taking the bait. Your response should pivot the conversation from what you are leaving to where you are going! It is all about reframing the question.

So you might respond:

"I am happy in my current position*, but I am looking for__(something this new job provides).

*Whether this is true or not

Do not get negative! If anything you says sounds, smells or tastes negative, stop, regroup and start again with a positive tone.

Remember when we talked about running to something, and not running from something?

WHEN YOU NEED MORE LOVE AND MORE MONEY

Let's use Robert as an example.

He's a political science lecturer at a major university in the Midwest. He had been an energy lobbyist until the 9/11 disaster and the Enron bankruptcy put him out of work.

He went back to school to get his master's degree in political science and landed a lecturer position at the university he had attended. His pay is very low. He has been teaching the same classes for many years, and his ego has taken a bruising.

He is the kind of guy who really likes a pat on the back from his bosses, which he does not receive. He gets appreciation from his students, but not from anyone else at the school.

The tedium of teaching the same classes has gotten to him. He has realized he needs a lot of variety to keep him motivated.

He needs to make more money. He is married with two kids, and the money is not sufficient. He is not on a tenure track, so this is somewhat of a dead-end job.

He wants a position as an energy lobbyist.

How could Robert respond when posed with the magic question on why he is leaving? One possible response could be:

"I love my job and my students, but what I really want is a position where I can get some recognition for my work, where I get to work on a wide variety of topics and I can make enough money to support my family."

Let's say the interview comes back with this: "Do you not get that from your current position?"

Robert could respond:

"My salary is of public record and you can look that up. I am focused on where I want to go, and your position seems to meet my criteria. Can I ask you about the variety of topics I would be working on at this position?"

He can pivot the response to where he is going and, when questioned, use it as a way to pose a question back to the interviewer.

Robert is focused on what he wants and is not going to take the bait!

Practice this yourself. Can you be prepared to pivot back with a question?

WHEN YOU NEED MORE STATUS AND MORE FREEDOM

Let's talk about James this time.

He works for a huge insurance company as director of HR, responsible for managing the medical benefits. He has been climbing the corporate ladder with a plan to be a VP. He is not happy in his current position working for a huge, slow-moving organization.

He has worked for medium size companies where he has had a leadership role in HR.

His boss Steve, VP of HR, whom James just adored, left because Steve's boss was a workaholic and expected all of his staff to be the same way.

After much thought, James has decided he would rather work for a smaller company again. He wants to be a big fish in small pond.

He has applied and is interviewing for Steve's old VP position but cannot see himself working for the workaholic boss. If offered the job, he will be put in a very difficult position because he has a family and wants a personal life.

He is also interviewing to become director of HR for a small/medium size company that is growing rapidly. He would have a small staff but would be responsible for the HR for the entire company.

When he interviews with this company, how should James answer the question "Why do you want to leave your current position?"

One response could be:

"I want to work for a smaller company where I can have an impact on all phases of HR within the company. I want to work in a dynamic environment. Can we talk about the new initiatives that are planned for the coming year?"

James did not answer the question but stated where he wanted to go, which hinted at why he might be leaving.

He immediately pivoted the conversation to a topic he wanted to discuss. Whenever you are posed with a question that has bait attached, deflect the bait and pivot the conversation back the other way.

WHEN YOU NEED TO BE
IN CHARGE OF THE PROCESS

For the third, and last, scenario we have Mary.

Mary works for a very large technology company in marketing operations. She is very good at her job. She likes to be able to control her schedule. Her current job is completely interruption- driven, which drives her nuts! Mary needs to work in an environment where she knows who is in control. She has had a new manager every six months for the last three years. Not good!

Mary has a very high social service interest; she likes to help people. She coaches girls' soccer teams and just loves it. She has networked her way into a smaller organization where she has applied for an HR position.

How should Mary answer when she's asked why she wants to leave her current role? One response could be:

"I want to take my operations skills and transition them into a position where I can have an impact on people's lives. I want a stable work and management environment. How long have you been the manager of this team, and how would you describe your management style?"

She asked for what she wanted and immediately pivoted the conversation back to the interviewer.

Mary should not say that she dislikes being interruption-driven or that she dislikes that her manager changes every six months. It is her responsibility to ask enough questions to find out whether the environment is to her liking.

I cannot state this enough: Interviewing is like dating and marriage! Both sides need to come prepared to find out whether there's a match.

ACTION STEPS:

✓ Formulate a positive-sounding response to the question "Why do you want to leave your current position?"

✓ Practice answering uncomfortable questions by asking the interviewer a question.

✓ Avoid saying anything that looks, smells or sounds even the least bit negative!

For additional resources, check out:

Repurpose Your Career Resource Center
https://careerpivot.com/RYC-Resources/

TIME TO ROLL UP YOUR SLEEVES

Let's face it: It would be great if we could snap our fingers and — poof! — we have a new career, a better body, a fatter retirement account and the ability to undo some of our history. While you can't undo your past, you can use what you've learned to make a better future.

Reviewing your past jobs, looking at what makes you happy, building a tribe ... all these tasks take time. Whatever your personality, talents or temperament, you're going to run into something along the way that really challenges you. For me, it was asking for help. For some people, it might be taking on social media, facing a truth in one's assessment or just being on the bottom of the totem pole again. That's all right: Being challenged can be a good thing.

Don't give up. As we've all acknowledged, retirement at 65 is no longer a reality for most people. You have decades ahead of you that you'll spend working. Isn't it worthwhile to invest some time now to create work you can enjoy? I know I'll probably be working the rest of my life. But I'd like it to be doing something I like for fewer hours than I used to spend at the office.

126

Be methodical. You can't make all these changes at once. Start with understanding yourself, your history and your needs. Then work from there. If you want more help or guidance, check out the Repurpose Your Career Resource Center https://careerpivot.com/RYC-Resources/I also take on individual clients with packages that range from short assessments of where they are to a long-term commitment to reach that final destination.

Make me part of your tribe!

Thanks for letting me share my journey with you. I wish you the best of everything in your search for a career that will grow with you!

ABOUT THE AUTHORS

Marc Miller's career journey included 22 years at IBM, several thriving tech startups, a painful stint as a high school teacher, a gig raising funds for the Jewish Community Association of Austin and a near-fatal bicycle accident that changed his perspective forever.

Thirty years of wandering the proverbial career desert, often repeating the same mistakes over and over, taught him his most crucial lesson: Most people don't really know what makes them happy at their core and what fulfills them. They pursue money, status, a skill set — all of which do provide some level of satisfaction— but not contentment. They wind up feeling frustrated and trapped. Others have figured out what they need, but don't know how to chart a course to get there.

An active member of the Launch Pad Job Club, Marc found himself counseling friends and associates on their career journeys and finally realized he'd found his vocation. He would use his extensive training experience to help others — especially Baby Boomers — find careers that they could grow into for the decades that lie ahead.

Marc is passionate about his work and the clients he serves. He's taught in more than 35 countries and helped clients from many industries.

Susan Lahey has always been passionate about words — as a medium — and stories. Especially true stories about ordinary people plucking up the courage to do something new and overcome obstacles, which describes Marc Miller and the clients he serves.

She grew up in the newsroom of The Kansas City Star and has freelanced for many publications on topics ranging from business and technology to art and sustainability. She has ghostwritten and co-written several books on personal development and finding meaningful work.

Made in the USA
Middletown, DE
17 September 2018